Number 125
Spring 2010

New Directions for Eva  **W9-BNL-321**

Sandra Mathison
Editor-in-Chief

The Systematic Screening and Assessment Method: Finding Innovations Worth Evaluating

Laura C. Leviton
Laura Kettel Khan
Nicola Dawkins
Editors

THE SYSTEMATIC SCREENING AND ASSESSMENT METHOD: FINDING
INNOVATIONS WORTH EVALUATING
Laura C. Leviton, Laura Kettel Khan, and Nicola Dawkins (eds.)
New Directions for Evaluation, no. 125
Sandra Mathison, Editor-in-Chief

Microfilm copies of issues and articles are available in 16mm and 35mm,
as well as microfiche in 105mm, through University Microfilms Inc., 300
North Zeeb Road, Ann Arbor, Michigan 48106-1346.

New Directions for Evaluation is indexed in Cambridge Scientific Abstracts
(CSA/CIG), Contents Pages in Education (T & F), Educational Research
Abstracts Online (T & F), ERIC Database (Education Resources
Information Center), Higher Education Abstracts (Claremont Graduate
University), Social Services Abstracts (CSA/CIG), Sociological Abstracts
(CSA/CIG), and Worldwide Political Sciences Abstracts (CSA/CIG).

NEW DIRECTIONS FOR EVALUATION (ISSN 1097-6736, electronic ISSN
1534-875X) is part of The Jossey-Bass Education Series and is published
quarterly by Wiley Subscription Services, Inc., A Wiley Company, at
Jossey-Bass, 989 Market Street, San Francisco, California 94103-1741.

SUBSCRIPTIONS cost $85 for U.S./Canada/Mexico; $109 international.
For institutions, agencies, and libraries, $256 U.S.; $296 Canada/Mexico;
$330 international. Prices subject to change.

EDITORIAL CORRESPONDENCE should be addressed to the Editor-in-Chief,
Sandra Mathison, University of British Columbia, 2125 Main Mall,
Vancouver, BC V6T 1Z4, Canada.

www.josseybass.com

Editorial Policy and Procedures

New Directions for Evaluation, a quarterly sourcebook, is an official publication of the American Evaluation Association. The journal publishes empirical, methodological, and theoretical works on all aspects of evaluation. A reflective approach to evaluation is an essential strand to be woven through every issue. The editors encourage issues that have one of three foci: (1) craft issues that present approaches, methods, or techniques that can be applied in evaluation practice, such as the use of templates, case studies, or survey research; (2) professional issues that present topics of import for the field of evaluation, such as utilization of evaluation or locus of evaluation capacity; (3) societal issues that draw out the implications of intellectual, social, or cultural developments for the field of evaluation, such as the women's movement, communitarianism, or multiculturalism. A wide range of substantive domains is appropriate for *New Directions for Evaluation;* however, the domains must be of interest to a large audience within the field of evaluation. We encourage a diversity of perspectives and experiences within each issue, as well as creative bridges between evaluation and other sectors of our collective lives.

The editors do not consider or publish unsolicited single manuscripts. Each issue of the journal is devoted to a single topic, with contributions solicited, organized, reviewed, and edited by a guest editor. Issues may take any of several forms, such as a series of related chapters, a debate, or a long article followed by brief critical commentaries. In all cases, the proposals must follow a specific format, which can be obtained from the editor-in-chief. These proposals are sent to members of the editorial board and to relevant substantive experts for peer review. The process may result in acceptance, a recommendation to revise and resubmit, or rejection. However, the editors are committed to working constructively with potential guest editors to help them develop acceptable proposals.

Sandra Mathison, Editor-in-Chief
University of British Columbia
2125 Main Mall
Vancouver, BC V6T 1Z4
CANADA
e-mail: nde@eval.org

CONTENTS

EDITORS' NOTES

This issue of *New Directions for Evaluation* describes the Systematic Screening and Assessment (SSA) Method, an innovative combination of existing evaluation methods. The method is a cost-effective strategy to identify real-world innovations that have promise of effectiveness. The focus of this issue is methodology, with abundant *practical* description of its application in childhood obesity prevention.

SSA assists program funders, practitioners, and researchers in selecting the most promising innovations already in use and then preparing them for further, more rigorous evaluation. It is a six-step process of:

1. Selecting a topic or theme
2. Soliciting nominations of innovations that address the theme
3. Using an expert panel to screen these nominations for those most plausible to meet criteria for promise
4. Conducting evaluability assessments on the nominations that pass this screen
5. Expert panel review of the evaluability assessment reports
6. Using the information, through three distinct products:
   A. Identifying the innovations that are most promising and ready for evaluation
   B. Providing constructive feedback to the innovators for program development
   C. Cluster synthesis of innovations that all reflect a similar program type

As seen in Chapter 1, the SSA Method is now being applied to several topics, but the application described in this issue was its first real test: to identify policy and environmental interventions likely to prevent childhood obesity.

Context: Childhood Obesity Prevention

This issue describes application of the SSA Method over a 2-year period in a collaborative project of the Robert Wood Johnson Foundation (RWJF), the

---

Note: The findings and conclusions presented are those of the authors and do not necessarily represent the official position of the agencies.

Centers for Disease Control and Prevention (CDC), and the CDC Foundation. The project, entitled the Early Assessment of Programs and Policies to Prevent Childhood Obesity, was funded by RWJF. ICF Macro served as the primary contractor and trainer of a distributed network of public health researchers and practitioners. With $2.6 million, this project examined 458 innovations over two years, in the areas of practice, programs, and local policies that affect children's environment. The project identified 20 innovations that are deemed *plausible* in producing large effects on children's diet or physical activity, are feasible to implement, reach a meaningful population of children, and meet other criteria (described in Chapters 1 and 2) for changing the prevalence of childhood obesity at a population level.

The last decade has seen an alarming rise in the proportion of children who are overweight and obese. This is especially true for low-income, African American, and Hispanic and Native American children, and for some children of Asian and Pacific Island heritage (Koplan, Liverman, & Kraak, 2001). Overweight and obesity are caused by an imbalance of calories consumed (diet) to calories expended (physical activity). Prevention of childhood obesity is different from treatment in that consistent, daily, but relatively minor changes are needed in calorie consumption or physical activity. Treatment of childhood obesity, in contrast, requires major lifestyle changes (Wang, Gortmaker, Sobol, & Kuntz, 2006).

RWJF is committed to reversing the epidemic of childhood obesity through prevention. The CDC, the National Institutes of Health (NIH), and the U.S. Department of Agriculture (USDA) are similarly committed, but for all age groups. RWJF and CDC have chosen as a special emphasis interventions that focus on the environment for eating and physical activity, and on the policies that affect the environment. Children's environment dictates whether healthy or unhealthy food will be offered to them, and the environment either enables or precludes time that they spend in physical activity.

We believe that the environment offers a powerful influence on behavior, because of our experience in controlling tobacco and other drugs. A policy and environmental approach, if properly implemented, can be more effective and sustainable than conventional health promotion strategies. These conventional strategies usually focus either on changing knowledge through education (a strategy that is largely ineffective in preventing childhood obesity) or at most they focus on individual, one-on-one behavior change. For several prevention problems, a one-on-one approach has been found to be less cost-effective than strategies that target entire populations at risk (Leviton, 1996).

Approaches that focus on policy and environmental changes may be effective in preventing childhood obesity. Policy and environmental interventions can focus on increasing physical activity; some possibilities are walkable neighborhoods, safe parks, and daily physical education in schools. Policy and environmental interventions can also focus on increased access to, and palatability of, less-calorie-dense foods, while limiting access to calorie-dense foods of limited nutritional value. Some possibilities are increasing access to fresh fruit and vegetables in low-income neighborhoods, or changing the offerings in the school cafeteria to limit access to sugar-sweetened beverages. Interventions can focus on policy or nonpolicy levers for environmental change and at any level: federal, state, local, or organizational (French, Story, & Jeffery, 2001; Kettel Khan et al., 2009; Parker, Burns, & Sanchez, 2009).

This focus presents two challenges, however. The evidence base for environmental and policy interventions in childhood obesity is limited at this early stage in development (Koplan et al., 2001). Although a great many studies report associations between environmental factors and childhood obesity, the causal evidence for their effects is still not satisfactory in most cases. At the same time, communities and schools are implementing a wide variety of interventions without much guidance as to effective practices. Literally hundreds of environmental interventions are being implemented across the country. This is seen in:

- Numerous new state legislative bills and laws (Dodson et al., 2009)
- The activities of the Healthy Eating Active Living Convergence Partnership, which includes RWJF, CDC, the Kellogg and Kresge foundations, the California Endowment, Kaiser Permanente, and Nemours Health and Preventive Services; http://www.convergencepartnership.org/site/c.fhLOK6PELmF/b.3917581/k.56AD/National_Partnership.htm
- The activities of state and local health departments (Association of State and Territorial Health Officials, 2008; National Association of County and City Health Officials, 2007)
- State and local school policies (Chriqui, Schneider, Chaloupka, Ide, & Pugach, 2009)
- Federal activities, such as CDC state-level cooperative agreements on physical activity and nutrition (Yee et al., 2006), the NIH focus on measurement of policy and environment for epidemiological assessment and evaluation of change (Story et al., 2009), and the USDA's implementation of electronic benefits transfer cards for the purchase of farmers' market products (USDA, 2009)

Out of this rich stew of activity and creativity, our guess was that at least some policy and environmental interventions were emerging that held promise of effectiveness. The challenge was to separate the wheat from the chaff efficiently through a process of using successive screens for plausible promise. The result was the Systematic Screening and Assessment Method.

The Rest of This Issue

In Chapter 1, Laura C. Leviton and Marjorie A. Gutman make the methods case for the SSA, contrast it with related evaluation practices, and describe important challenges encountered at each step from an *evaluator's* point of view. In Chapter 2, Nicola Dawkins and her colleagues describe in detail the operation of the SSA Method as applied to the 2-year RWJF/CDC/Macro Early Assessment initiative to identify the most promising innovations in childhood obesity prevention. In addition, Chapter 2 describes in detail the yield from this initiative, in terms of promising innovations that are also ready for evaluation. In Chapter 3, Thearis Osuji and her colleagues describe training and field support for the conduct of 48 evaluability assessments, the centerpiece of the SSA Method. Chapter 4 consists of three in-depth case studies in which Seraphine Pitt Barnes, Holly Wethington, and Karen Cheung each describe the process of assessing an innovation selected during the first year of the initiative's operation. In Chapter 5, Laura Kettel Khan and her colleagues reflect on how the SSA Method has influenced the field of childhood obesity prevention as well as public health practice, and they speculate about how the SSA may inform evaluation practice. Finally, in Chapter 6, Debra J. Rog reflects on the SSA Method as a novel way to use evaluability assessment.

To our knowledge, nothing similar to the SSA Method has been attempted before, although several efforts informed its creation. Veteran evaluation professionals have corroborated this. Of course, nothing is brand new under the sun, and the SSA represents merely a new combination of existing techniques. In Chapter 1, we compare and contrast the method to related efforts. In the final analysis, it is for the reader to judge whether the Systematic Screening and Assessment Method offers value to evaluation.

References

Association of State and Territorial Health Officials. (2008). *Position statement: Obesity prevention and control.* Arlington, VA: Author. Retrieved September 25, 2009, from http://astho.dev.networkats.com/page.aspx?id=765&terms=%22obesity

Chriqui, J. F., Schneider, L., Chaloupka, F. J., Ide, K., & Pugach, O. (2009). *Local wellness policies: Assessing school district strategies for improving children's health. School years 2006–07 and 2007–08.* Chicago: Bridging the Gap, Health Policy Center, Institute for Health Research and Policy, University of Illinois at Chicago.

Dodson, E. A., Fleming, C., Boehmer, T. K., Haire-Joshu, D., Luke, D. A., & Brownson, R. C. (2009). Preventing childhood obesity through state policy: Qualitative assessment of enablers and barriers. *Journal of Public Health Policy, 30,* S161–S176.

French, S. A., Story, M., & Jeffery, R. W. (2001). Environmental influences on eating and physical activity. *Annual Review of Public Health, 22,* 309–335.

Kettel Khan, L., Sobush, K., Keener, D., Goodman, K., Lowry, A., Kakietek, J., et al. (2009). Recommended community strategies and measurements to prevent obesity in the United States. *MMWR, 58*(RR07), 1–26.

Koplan, J. P., Liverman, C. T., & Kraak, V. I. (Eds.). (2001). *Preventing childhood obesity: Health in the balance.* Washington, DC: National Academies Press.

Leviton, L. C. (1996). Integrating psychology and public health: Challenges and opportunities. *American Psychologist, 51*(1), 42–51.

National Association of County and City Health Officials. (2007). *Statement of policy supporting efforts in the prevention and treatment of obesity and overweight.* Washington, DC:

Author. Retrieved September 25, 2009, from http://www.naccho.org/advocacy/positions/upload/Res04–02Obesity.pdf

Parker, L., Burns, A. C., & Sanchez, E. (Eds.). (2009). *Local government actions to prevent childhood obesity*. Washington, DC: National Academies Press.

Story, M., Giles-Corti, B., Yaroch, A. L., Cummins, S., Frank, L. D., Huang, T.T.-K., et al. (2009). Work Group IV: Future directions for measures of the food and physical activity environments. *American Journal of Preventive Medicine, 36*(4S), S182–S188.

USDA. (2009). Agriculture Secretary Vilsack announces 86 grants under the Farmers Market Promotion Program. News Release no. 0451.09. Retrieved September 25, 2009, from http://www.usda.gov/wps/portal/!ut/p/_s.7_0_A/7_0_1OB?contentidonly=true&contentid=2009/09/0451.xml

Wang, Y. C., Gortmaker, S. L., Sobol, A. M., & Kuntz, K. M. (2006). Estimating the energy gap among U.S. children: A counterfactual approach. *Pediatrics, 118*(6), e1721–e1733.

Yee, S. L., Williams-Piehota, P., Sorensen, A., Roussel, A., Hersey, J., & Hamre, R. (2006). The Nutrition and Physical Activity Program to Prevent Obesity and Other Chronic Diseases: Monitoring progress in funded states. *Preventing Chronic Disease* [serial online] Vol. 3. Retrieved September 25, 2009, from http://www.cdc.gov/pcd/issues/2006/jan/05_0077.htm

Laura C. Leviton
Laura Kettel Khan
Nicola Dawkins
Editors

LAURA C. LEVITON is the coauthor of Foundations of Program Evaluation *and is currently Special Advisor for Evaluation at the Robert Wood Johnson Foundation, where for the past 10 years she has overseen more than 80 evaluations at the national, state, and local levels.*

LAURA KETTEL KHAN is currently the Senior Scientist for Policy and Partnerships in the Division of Nutrition, Physical Activity, and Obesity at the Centers for Disease Control and Prevention (CDC), the primary public health agency working to prevent obesity and chronic diseases in the United States.

NICOLA DAWKINS is a Principal of ICF Macro where she designs and implements research and evaluation studies and led Macro's team in coordinating the Robert Wood Johnson Foundation/CDC initiative Early Assessment of Programs and Policies to Prevent Childhood Obesity.

Leviton, L. C., & Gutman, M. A. (2010). Overview and rationale for the Systematic Screen-
ing and Assessment Method. In L. C. Leviton, L. Kettel Khan, & N. Dawkins (Eds.), *The
Systematic Screening and Assessment Method: Finding innovations worth evaluating. New
Directions for Evaluation, 125*, 7–31.

1

Overview and Rationale for the Systematic Screening and Assessment Method

Laura C. Leviton, Marjorie A. Gutman

Abstract

*This chapter gives the rationale and conceptual defense for the Systematic
Screening and Assessment (SSA) Method, a way to identify the most promising
innovations in preparation for rigorous evaluation. The SSA Method starts by
identifying the innovations that real-world practitioners have developed and then
systematically assesses which innovations will offer the greatest payoff from further evaluation. Through sequential purchase of evaluative information, the SSA
Method aims to avoid a variety of problems that evaluators encounter in studying innovations. Besides the identification of promising innovations for evaluation, the benefits include expert technical assistance and feedback to innovators,
cross-site syntheses of trends and common practices, and cost efficiency compared to evaluating innovations that have not been selected or screened for
promise.* © Wiley Periodicals, Inc., and the American Evaluation Association.

The Systematic Screening and Assessment (SSA) Method identifies for
evaluation the practice-based innovations that are most likely to be
effective, thus increasing the potential for productive outcome evaluation. The SSA Method does this by improving the prior information about

these innovations' plausibility for impact, feasibility, and readiness for evaluation. The most promising innovations then receive the highest priority for outcome evaluation resources. SSA is also useful for informing the field about prevalent practices and providing constructive feedback and technical assistance to innovators. However, its primary purpose is to prepare the way to evaluate the effectiveness of practice-based innovations and disseminate their models for adoption elsewhere.

We believe the SSA Method is a new and important addition to the methods available to evaluate innovations. However, there are so many unjustified claims about new evaluation practices that we need to be careful to justify exactly what is new about this one. The method is new in that it sequences two existing evaluation methods, namely evaluability assessment (Wholey, 1979, 2004) and connoisseurship or expert judgment (Rossi, Lipsey, & Freeman, 2003). By sequencing these methods, the SSA Method creates a systematic process for nominating, screening, and assessing promising innovations. As discussed later, SSA joins a family of emerging methods to translate practice into research by focusing evaluation attention on strategies and interventions that are currently being undertaken by practitioners (Glasgow, Green, et al., 2006).

The chapters in this issue of *New Directions for Evaluation* describe application of the Systematic Screening and Assessment Method to childhood obesity prevention in a 2-year initiative titled the Early Assessment of Programs and Policies to Prevent Childhood Obesity (the Early Assessment initiative). The Robert Wood Johnson Foundation (RWJF) funded the initiative and the Centers for Disease Control and Prevention (CDC) directed it. ICF Macro served as the coordinating center, trained 40 professionals in the conduct of evaluability assessments, and conducted 48 evaluability assessments.

Childhood obesity is not the only application of the SSA. The first year results of the Early Assessment project led to three other efforts to identify innovations worth evaluating, in nursing education (Rutgers University with funding by RWJF), programs to address intimate partner violence in immigrant populations (LTG Associates with funding by RWJF), and heart disease and stroke prevention (CDC and ICF Macro).

Overview of the SSA Method

Figure 1.1 summarizes the six-step Systematic Review and Assessment Method.

Step 1: Selection of priority areas for assessment, to focus a scan of innovations. Ideally, the priority areas for studying innovations should be selected in conjunction with key stakeholders and potential users. The Early Assessment initiative selected five such priority areas in consultation with federal stakeholders and experts: school district local wellness policies, day care and after-school settings, access to healthy food in poor communities,

Figure 1.1. The Systematic Review and Assessment Method

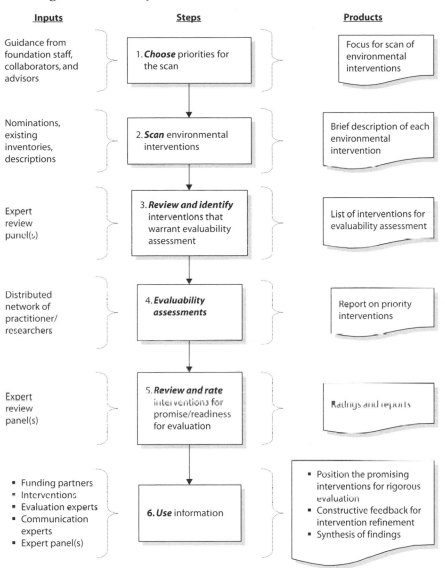

Inputs	Steps	Products
Guidance from foundation staff, collaborators, and advisors	1. **Choose** priorities for the scan	Focus for scan of environmental interventions
Nominations, existing inventories, descriptions	2. **Scan** environmental interventions	Brief description of each environmental intervention
Expert review panel(s)	3. **Review and identify** interventions that warrant evaluability assessment	List of interventions for evaluability assessment
Distributed network of practitioner/ researchers	4. **Evaluability assessments**	Report on priority interventions
Expert review panel(s)	5. **Review and rate** interventions for promise/readiness for evaluation	Ratings and reports
• Funding partners • Interventions • Evaluation experts • Communication experts • Expert panel(s)	6. **Use** information	• Position the promising interventions for rigorous evaluation • Constructive feedback for intervention refinement • Synthesis of findings

comprehensive school-based physical activity programs, and features of the built environment that facilitate physical activity. They were chosen because relatively little is known about them, yet they are prevalent and have high potential leverage for changing policy and environmental conditions that affect childhood obesity.

Step 2: Scan of innovations in those priority areas. The SSA Method requires a way to identify a high volume of innovations, either through nomination or other alternatives (described below). In the Early Assessment initiative, we asked a wide range of public health professionals and policy makers for nominations in the priority areas. The CDC staff obtained 458 nominations over the 2-year period, of which 174 met inclusion criteria and 128 were summarized for step 3.

Step 3: Initial review of innovations by an expert panel. In SSA, the initial list of innovations is screened to further select those that have potential promise using explicit, mutually agreed criteria. Experts rated the plausibility of:

- Potential impact
- Reach to cover the target population
- Feasibility of adoption by similar organizations
- Generalizability
- Staff and organizational capacity to undergo and use evaluability assessment

The innovations that meet these criteria are then scheduled for evaluability assessment (EA). In the Early Assessment initiative, we created a panel of content experts and evaluation professionals who reviewed documentation on the selected, nominated programs and policies. The panel reviewed 128 of the innovations and recommended 53 of them for EA.

Step 4: Evaluability assessment of the selected innovations. For each innovation selected by expert judges in the SSA Method, an EA is conducted to elicit a program description that includes a logic model and theory of change, articulates the expectations of stakeholders, and helps us better understand the reality of program resources and activities (Leviton, Kettel Khan, Rog, Dawkins, & Cotton, in press; Wholey, 1979, 2004). On this basis we can further understand the innovations' plausibility for effectiveness and feasibility of adoption in other settings. In the Early Assessment initiative, ICF Macro staff trained a distributed network of researchers and public health professionals in EA, which then conducted an EA on each innovation. Innovators generally welcomed these assessments: of the 53 selected for EA, all but 5 participated and 2 of these refusals were unrelated to their interest in participating.

Step 5: Second expert panel review of the assessed innovations. In the SSA Method, the expert judges review the innovations a second time using the evaluability assessment reports to further reduce uncertainty about their promise, feasibility, and readiness for more rigorous evaluation. In the Early Assessment initiative, evaluability assessment reports were reviewed for 48 innovations, of which 33 were ready for more formal evaluation. The expert panel deemed 20 of these to be highly promising for *substantial* impact at a population level and identified 6 of them as having the highest priority for evaluation.

Step 6: Use of information. The SSA Method results in three distinct uses of information derived from the process. First, *the most promising innovations are positioned for rigorous evaluation.* These are the expert panel's top priorities in terms of likely impact, reach, feasibility, generalizability, and potential information payoff. Funders may proceed immediately with full evaluation of the top priorities, or further planning and preparation may be required. The Early Assessment initiative identified 6 top priorities for evaluation: in 2009, evaluation was under way for 3 of these and another 2 were approved for funding. In addition, a variety of funders are considering evaluation of the remaining 15 innovations found to be both highly promising and ready for evaluation.

Second, *the developers and managers* of the innovations that undergo evaluability assessments *receive tailored, constructive feedback* about program operations on the basis of the evaluability assessments. In the Early Assessment initiative, feedback also included content expertise from CDC experts in physical activity and nutrition. As seen in Chapters 2 and 3, innovators found this feedback useful.

Third, after reviewing a high volume of innovations, we get *a sense of the field in question.* All the innovations that are screened and reviewed, whether promising or not, reveal a great deal about the types of projects being undertaken, their prevalence and popularity, and their facilitators, obstacles, and fatal flaws. Chapter 5 describes the utility of this information in the Early Assessment initiative, as do synthesis reports on the topics of focus, which will soon be posted by CDC at the following index: http://www.cdc.gov/nccdphp/dnpao (Cheung, Dawkins, Kettel Khan & Leviton, 2009; Pitt Barnes, Robin, Dawkins, Leviton, & Kettel Khan, 2009a, 2009b; Skelton, Dawkins, Leviton, & Kettel Khan, 2009; Wethington, Kirkconnell Hall, Dawkins, Leviton, & Kettel Khan, 2009).

Why This Combination of Steps?

The methods employed in SSA have all been used before, but alone or in isolated pairings. By combining them systematically, the SSA Method stretches limited evaluation resources by identifying innovations with promise for effectiveness. Combining these nomination, expert rating, and assessment activities in a seamless screening process, SSA aims to:

- Avoid wasting precious resources on a "no effect" conclusion (Wholey, 1979)
- Prevent the chilling effect that a premature negative evaluation can have on innovations to combat childhood obesity (Shadish, Cook, & Leviton, 1991; Weiss, 1987)
- Provide useful formative feedback to projects for a low cost and low response burden, optimizing their further development (Carman & Fredericks, 2008; Leviton et al., in press; Smith, 1989)
- Prepare the highest-priority innovations for rigorous evaluation of effectiveness (Cook, Leviton, & Shadish, 1985)

- Offer timely insights to the field and funding organizations on the range of innovations, their strengths, and limitations (Cheung et al., 2009; Pitt Barnes et al., 2009a, 2009b; Skelton et al., 2009; Wethington et al., 2009)

Once we have identified the innovations that are most promising and ready for evaluation, the logical next step (and the primary reason for the SSA Method) is to evaluate their effectiveness. RWJF and the CDC are taking this step for five of the six highest-priority innovations from the first year of the Early Assessment initiative. In addition, the rest of the innovations that were deemed promising and ready for evaluation are being considered for development and test by a variety of other funders and researchers interested in these issues.

Rationale for the SSA Method

We developed the SSA Method to address a dilemma in evaluation. Society expects evaluation to identify effective innovations, but society seems to spend a lot of money evaluating innovations that turn out not to be effective. Some innovations may have been well conceived but ultimately ineffective; others may be less well-conceived, or they may be implemented with inadequate consistency or intensity. Even with those that are deemed effective, front-line practitioners may find them not feasible to employ. This situation serves neither evaluation nor the society that supports it very well.

To address this problem, the SSA Method relies on five assumptions:

1. Practitioners and policy makers are developing many innovations to address a problem, such as childhood obesity.
2. At least some of these innovations may be effective.
3. Because practitioners developed the innovations, they are likely to be feasible for implementation in real-world situations.
4. Using the principle of sequential purchase of information (Wholey, 1979), we can screen a high volume of these innovations at relatively low cost.
5. Through the SSA Method, we can reduce uncertainty about which innovations are likely to be effective and feasible, and therefore appropriate for full evaluation.

Where these assumptions hold, we can capitalize on the variety of practice-based innovations at the same time that we preserve scarce evaluation resources to test the innovations that are most worth evaluating.

Evaluating Innovations: An Uncertain Endeavor. In the face of any new social problem, practitioners, organizations, and policy makers attempt a variety of innovations. In this sense, societal innovation is an adaptive mechanism; it produces variation, some of which may be effective in dealing with the social problem. When a new problem presents itself, one can expect to see a lot of innovation, through both practice and research. Certainly this is the case in childhood obesity prevention, where neither research nor practice has yet developed sufficiently to offer good solutions (Koplan, Liverman, & Kraak, 2001). At the Robert Wood Johnson Foundation and at the Centers for Disease Control, evaluators have taken a front row seat to observe the many innovations and solutions that are put forth. But as funders we must ask, Which of these innovations should be further developed and tested for effectiveness?

In principle, evaluation serves a useful function as a selection mechanism to establish which variants are effective. Donald Campbell (1977) related this process to the philosophical concept of evolutionary epistemology, in which trial-and-error learning permits us to discover reliable causal relationships (Shadish et al., 1991). In the case of childhood obesity prevention, we would like to fund rigorous evaluation to assess the effectiveness, reach, and feasibility of the innovations that are put forth. But which of the many innovations should be evaluated? Resources do not permit an adequate test of each and every innovation. Like most evaluators and funders, we want to increase the probability that the innovations we evaluate turn out to be effective and have leverage to produce change in many places.

Unfortunately, evaluation as normally practiced does not make cost-effective use of evaluation resources to identify effective innovations. In evaluation practice of *all* varieties, the client (a funder, an organization, or a participatory coalition) usually presents the evaluator with a given innovation to be evaluated. Obviously, the client believes there is a reasonable likelihood that the innovation is effective, thinking this ideally on the basis of some prior information. The prior information can come from experience, literature review, program theory, management information, available data, or evaluation. All too often, however, prior information is very limited as to an innovation's maturity, stability, and plausible effectiveness. Sadly, evaluation of such an innovation has a high likelihood of reaching a no-effect conclusion. Influential evaluation writers have spoken to why this might be the case (Lipsey, 1988; Reichert, 1994; Wholey, 1979; Wilson & Lipsey, 2001). Sometimes a no-effect conclusion can be valuable (Henry, 2003). However, in our experience many programs with no-effect conclusions could have been established as ineffective using much-less-costly methods than those employed in a conventional evaluation. Moreover, Weiss (1987) has noted that premature negative evaluation can have a chilling effect on innovation, leading to the assumption that nothing is effective, when in fact something might be effective to address the problem. In areas such as childhood obesity prevention, we cannot afford to discourage innovation—there is a serious need to reverse a disturbing national trend.

More Cost-Effective Evaluation of Innovations. One way to improve the likelihood of finding an effective innovation is to have a larger pool of potential innovations from which to choose for evaluation. In the SSA

Method, therefore, we begin by identifying as large an array of innovations as possible in a given area. However, testing all of them would be prohibitively expensive, and as seen below we have reason to believe that the yield from testing all such innovations would be small.

To ensure that the process yields more information in a more cost-effective manner, we borrowed from Wholey's (1979) principle of sequential purchase of information. Wholey coined this term to describe a more orderly process for producing useful evaluative information. By employing less expensive methods first, Wholey used information to further refine stakeholder questions, assess whether a program could indeed be evaluated, and also assess whether stakeholders would in fact use the information. In other words, less expensive information was used to reduce uncertainty about whether more expensive evaluation information would be useful (Cronbach, 1982).

In the SSA Method, we employ sequential purchase of information in a somewhat different way than Wholey and his colleagues did: to select from among many innovations those that have a good prior probability of having impact. Only if the initial phases of SSA indicate the promise of an innovation are we justified in collecting additional information. Thus expert judgment is used to determine whether evaluability assessment is warranted. Evaluability assessment is used to gather information about the project's promise and readiness for evaluation. A second expert judgment after the evaluability assessments is used to determine whether more expensive, rigorous evaluation of an innovation is warranted.

Making the Case for Cost-Effectiveness. To support our belief that the SSA Method is cost-effective, we invite the reader to participate in a simple thought experiment, or simulation. Examine the yield from the Early Assessment initiative as reported in Chapter 2, and then imagine the resources that would be required if formal evaluations of effectiveness were conducted on all of the nominated projects, or on any randomly selected project. Across the 2 years of the Early Assessment initiative, 458 policy and environmental innovations were nominated. Of these, 174 (38%) met inclusion criteria, meaning they were appropriate nominations (see Chapter 2). For various reasons, 128 of these appropriate nominations were presented to the expert panel for review. We budgeted for about 50 evaluability assessments, and the expert panel had few problems in identifying 53 that seemed the most promising to warrant inclusion. Of these, 48 innovations underwent evaluability assessment, 33 of these were ready for more formal evaluation and 20 of the innovations met our criteria for high promise and readiness for evaluation. Six of the innovations were judged to have the highest priority for formal evaluation. In other words, the yield from the initiative was that 4.4% of all nominations were deemed highly promising, between 11.5% and 15.6% of all appropriate nominations were viewed as promising, and 42% of the nominations that underwent evaluability assessment were both highly promising and ready for evaluation.

NEW DIRECTIONS FOR EVALUATION • DOI: 10.1002/ev

We should consider the yield from each of these steps in turn, starting with all 458 nominations. If only 4.4% of identifiable innovations in a new area of policy and programs are promising and therefore have even a reasonable likelihood of being effective, then this argues against a willy-nilly intensive evaluation of every innovation that is nominated. The cost of doing so would dwarf our capacity to implement these innovations, let alone study them. Evaluation of the innovations for other purposes— formative feedback, program improvement, monitoring—might be warranted if resources were available. But recall that the purpose of the SSA Method is to identify the most promising, highest-priority innovations for testing and potential spread.

Granted, 62% of the nominations in this initiative were not appropriate for one reason or another, and it might be feasible to narrow the focus for nominations to better select those that meet criteria. Nevertheless, someone decided that each and every one of the 458 innovations might be worth evaluating! Veteran evaluation practitioners will recognize a familiar pattern, because many of them have been asked to evaluate inappropriate innovations. Even in well-developed program areas, many programs undergo evaluation when they exist only on paper, or they require substantial development before summative evaluation would be appropriate (e.g., Lipsey, 1988; Reichert, 1994; Wholey, 1979, 2004).

Of course, a serious effort to study innovations would instead focus on the 174 appropriate nominations—provided they were recognized as such. An 11.5% yield of promising interventions, using appropriate nominations as the denominator looks much more optimistic than 4.4%. So does a 15.6% yield, considering that the expert panel reviewed only 128 of the appropriate nominations. We may also have missed a few promising projects in the transition from 174 to 128 innovations (see Chapter 2), so we might even inflate this percentage a bit. A CDC effort that preceded SSA identified 9 out of 41 projects as promising, so let us assume that between 15% and 25% of the appropriate nominations are likely to be promising. Yet even if 25% of innovations were promising and ready for evaluation, we would still argue that the SSA Method can save substantial evaluation resources and direct them to areas for the biggest payoff.

Here is our reasoning: of the $3 million RWJF/CDC initiative, $600,000 was reserved to conduct a formal evaluation of the highest-priority innovation identified in year one. Therefore the cost per innovation identified as highly promising and ready for evaluation, including all infrastructure, training, and technical assistance, was $2.4 million divided by 20, or $120,000. The SSA Method is cheap at that price; consider the many very expensive evaluations that have reached no-effect conclusions over the past 35 years! An adequate study of intervention effectiveness is at least $2 million, so if formal evaluation were conducted on all the eligible innovations, and one in four were both promising and ready for evaluation, we would have to spend at least $8 million in order to identify even one intervention that had a good chance of being found effective. Even if evaluations could be done on the cheap, at around $150,000 each, then to find interventions with even a hope of being effective we would have to spend at least $600,000 to identify one promising intervention, and to find all of them we would spend 174 times $150,000, or more than $26 million.

The same argument applies to the 48 innovations that underwent EA; 28 of them were either not promising or not ready for evaluation, so outcome evaluation would certainly be premature, and probably the evaluation of implementation as well, given that program development could be guided by the EAs as a first step (Smith, 1989). Among the 20 highly promising innovations that were ready for evaluation, expert judges were very clear that evaluating 6 of them would produce the biggest payoffs for childhood obesity prevention.

We are still underestimating the resources that would be needed if we evaluated unselected innovations to detect the effective ones. Wilson and Lipsey (2001) have demonstrated how the study conditions in practice-based settings reduce the obtained effect sizes from evaluations. Effect sizes decrease because the study conditions are not so well controlled, introducing problems of measurement, design, analysis, and treatment intensity. For these reasons, the probability of finding an effective intervention would be lower, and the actual cost per effective innovation would be substantially more than the amounts estimated in our thought experiment. It takes powerful interventions, like the six priorities identified by our expert panel, to overcome these conditions. A $120,000 expenditure to identify a highly promising innovation starts to look thrifty indeed compared to the general payoff from evaluation of innovations.

The cost per highly promising innovation does not take into account the other benefits deriving from the SSA Method, such as technical assistance and feedback to the developers and managers of the innovations (see Chapter 2), the five syntheses of knowledge about innovations or the improved evaluation capacity of public health (Chapter 5). As they stated in surveys, the innovators found the formative feedback to be useful (see Chapters 2 and 5). For technical assistance and feedback alone, disregarding identification of promising projects, the cost was $50,000 per innovation that underwent EA—a reasonably cost-effective format to improve development of promising innovations in a new area for which solutions are badly needed.

Comparison With Other Strategies to Test, Disseminate, and Replicate Innovations. A focus on evaluating innovations is not new, of course. Many federal agencies have undertaken the strategy of research, development, and dissemination (R&D) of programs and practices, including the U.S. Department of Education (n.d.; Katzenmeyer & Haertel,1986), the Substance Abuse and Mental Health Services Administration (2009), National Institute of Mental Health (2009; Davis & Salasin, 1975), the National Institutes of Health (2008), the Agency for Healthcare Research and Quality (2002), National Institute of Justice (2008), and the CDC (for HIV prevention, 2008). Generally these R&D programs solicit innovations that are evaluated for effectiveness and then disseminate the effective ones to practitioners.

These are extremely important initiatives, and we do not pretend that the SSA Method could replace them. However, the methods for soliciting innovations to undergo a test could be more systematic and cost-effective. We are not the first to make this observation (e.g., Cronbach, 1982). Consider the total amount of time, effort, and resources that were required for testing the innovations in these federal initiatives and then culling the ineffective ones. The total cost is daunting indeed. How many thousands of evaluations had to be conducted to identify the programs that are endorsed and disseminated by federal agencies? Would they have shortened the process by increasing the prior probability of selecting the most promising interventions, and ensuring that they could be evaluated?

By adapting the evaluation principle of sequential purchase of information, the SSA Method focuses on the innovations that are most likely to be effective and amenable to evaluation. In this way, the funders of evaluation can increase the chances that subsequent, more rigorous evaluation focuses on those programs and practices with the best promise of achieving the desired effects.

One might argue that the peer review process of research grant funding also represents a way to improve the probability that only the promising innovations will receive an evaluative test. Certainly, federal programs select many innovations this way. However, peer reviewers rely almost exclusively on paper documents and assurances about pilot tests. On occasion, site visits are made, but rarely does the process include reality testing of the kind represented by evaluability assessment.

Assuring Feasibility for Real-World Implementation. Conventional federal research and development initiatives rely on researchers to develop innovations that practitioners and program managers are then expected to adopt. This is the evidence-based practice model. One challenge to these efforts is that researchers often do not have a good conception of the constraints on practice in real-world settings. Program managers and practitioners repeatedly express concern that they cannot implement these innovations: they do not have the resources and time, or they must adapt the innovations to fit the needs of the setting. In some cases, the innovations may not be acceptable to the populations they aim to affect. These complaints arise chronically in areas as disparate as medical care quality (Berwick, 2003), community mental health (Davis & Salasin, 1975), AIDS prevention (Leviton & Guinan, 2003), and criminal justice and education (Emshoff et al., 1987). Although real-world organizations can indeed implement well-constructed programs with fidelity (Emshoff et al., 1987; Griffin et al., 2009), this issue still poses a constant challenge to the R&D model of innovation.

NEW DIRECTIONS FOR EVALUATION • DOI: 10.1002/ev

To address the problem of real-world implementation, Glasgow, Green, et al. (2006) have called for an effort to "translate practice into research" to identify and develop practices, programs, and policies that have proven feasible and acceptable in the real world of health and social services. This effort, the practice-based evidence model, would parallel the federal initiatives that rely on researchers to develop and disseminate innovations.

The SSA Method translates practice into research, because it starts with the premise that practitioners and program managers have themselves developed innovations worth investigating. Some relevant efforts have preceded this work. The school improvement literature offers examples (Teddie & Stringfield, 2007), as does the CDC SWAT initiative to be described here (Dunet et al., 2008; Hersey et al., 2008). RWJF has sometimes sought real-world practices for a test; for example, the Finding Answers national program solicits interventions on cardiac care for minority populations that then undergo evaluation and dissemination of those found to be effective (Schlotthauer et al., 2008).

Three cautions are in order about the focus on real-world practices. First, the SSA Method assumes that such innovations exist and at least some of them are likely to be effective. In the case of childhood obesity, this assumption is reasonable. However, other new social programming areas may not have much practice-based innovation, or the innovations that exist may not be sufficiently powerful to achieve the objective. If this were the case, then the R&D focus as employed in federal initiatives might be more appropriate than SSA, because researchers could apply existing behavioral and social theory to develop innovations. Nevertheless, SSA might be helpful because of its explicit focus on the theory of change and real-world assessment.

A second caution is that we assume innovations developed by practitioners are more likely to be implemented than those developed by researchers. This may not be the case for all innovations, however. Some researchers may develop innovations with practitioners in mind, and some practitioner-developed innovations may be so constrained by local circumstances as to be completely infeasible for replication elsewhere. In the case of childhood obesity, however, three of the top innovations identified through the SSA Method are already being adopted or considered for adoption by other policy makers and practitioners in the nation.

A third caution is perhaps most serious from an evaluation standpoint. SSA assumes that more rigorous evaluation will follow the selection of innovations through the six-step process. However, SSA may be misused; practitioners or decision makers could choose to disseminate the identified models without a proper evaluative test. This danger is exemplified by the many efforts to identify best practices in various program and policy sectors. By what standard do we regard these practices as "best"? The standards are sometimes good, sometimes not so good. At times, dissemination may be warranted without an evaluation, as when a body of evidence gives compelling support to the theory behind the best practice, or when common sense makes it patently obvious that the best practice should be disseminated. This was the case for the CDC SWAT initiative (to be described), in which high-quality studies of worksite obesity prevention had already been conducted. However, in a new field, or when innovations depart from existing evidence-based practice, it is not sufficient to disseminate best practices. SSA is explicit in its aim to subject promising approaches to a *rigorous* test.

Development of the SSA Method

The idea for the SSA Method originated in discussions between the first author and Thomas Cook in the early 1980s (Cook, Leviton, & Shadish, 1985). However, the idea was never implemented, to our knowledge or Cook's, perhaps because only a limited number of funders can implement it at the necessary scale. At RWJF, the timing was right to explore this idea as we tackled the question of how to prevent childhood obesity. The Institute of Medicine had recommended changing children's environments to prevent obesity: the availability of healthy foods, limits on access to unhealthy foods, and reintroducing opportunities for physical activity into children's lives (Koplan et al., 2001). To implement environmental changes often requires policy changes at the local, state, or federal level. Many localities and some states were beginning to innovate in creation of such policies; however, very little was known about their effectiveness. The SSA Method reemerged out of discussions of the need for more rapid identification of innovations that might be effective in preventing childhood obesity.

Three other initiatives informed development of SSA. They help to locate it within a family of methods that first identify promising programs and practices and then investigate them. First was the school improvement effort of the early 1980s, which identified schools that were performing better than would be predicted on the basis of their resources and the background of the children (Teddie & Stringfield, 2007). High-performing schools were selected either because of "outlier" status or consistently high performance year after year, controlling for these background characteristics. Investigators found consistent differences between these schools and lower-performing schools. However, independent outcome studies of any of these characteristics were extremely rare (Teddie & Stringfield, 2007). Unlike the outlier methods as applied to school improvement research, the SSA Method aimed specifically to plan for independent tests of the effectiveness of the promising exemplars. Nevertheless, the school improvement literature gave us confidence that we might identify promising practices using SSA.

A second initiative consisted of 27 EAs that RWJF funded from 2005 to 2007, on pilot projects on childhood obesity prevention. Three separate evaluation teams conducted these evaluability assessments so that we could get an idea of the diversity of approaches and findings (OMG Center for Collaborative Learning, 2007; Rhodes, 2007; Rog & Gutman, 2007). These EAs gave us a sense of the unit cost for third-party evaluability assessments, at about $35,000 per innovation studied. The cost can be lower; Leviton, Collins, Laird, and Kratt (1998) describe 25 EAs that master's of public health students conducted as service learning projects.

The third project was a CDC initiative, the Swift Worksite Assessment and Translation (SWAT) project. We need to give credit where credit is due: SWAT predated the Early Assessment initiative and employed many of the same principles. Indeed, it gave decision makers confidence to proceed with the Early Assessment initiative. The CDC SWAT project's goal was to develop a rapid assessment method that could investigate innovations being implemented in the field one at a time against a standard set of criteria. At the time of the SWAT project's initiation, much attention was being turned to obesity in various settings, including worksites, and CDC staff was being asked about the effectiveness of new interventions that had not been formally studied. In addition, some innovations spread rapidly, despite questionable appropriateness (such as public weigh-ins meant to shame employees into healthier behavior). Thus the need arose for a systematic way to quickly investigate an innovation and make a preliminary determination about its public health relevance and probable effectiveness in addressing obesity. In its developmental first round, the SWAT project identified 41 innovations of worksite obesity prevention and implemented 9 SWAT assessments in a "batchlike" approach in order to further refine SWAT (Dunet et al., 2008; Hersey et al, 2008). Even so, the intent was never to examine large groups of innovations together. The goal was strictly to assess programs one-at-a-time, in the same way as CDC's traditional public health "outbreak investigations."

During their developmental stages, the SSA and SWAT projects interacted extensively. At the recommendation of the first author (Leviton), the SWAT project employed evaluability assessment in site visits. The director of the SWAT project (Dunet) was directly involved in first-year implementation of the Early Assessment initiative and is a coauthor of Chapter 2.

There are several similarities between the SWAT approach and the SSA Method, but some notable differences as well. Like SSA, the SWAT project employed an initial search for innovations, using available publications, the Internet, and nominations. SWAT used evaluability assessment and expert judgment (although in a different sequence from SSA). Based on SWAT experience, the SSA Method included feedback and technical assistance to each innovation that received an EA. In a later section, we describe some notable differences and discuss some conditions under which SWAT might be preferable to the SSA Method. Certainly there were differences in use of findings.

NEW DIRECTIONS FOR EVALUATION • DOI: 10.1002/ev

To plan the Early Assessment initiative, RWJF invited expert advisors to review the proposed approach and offer suggestions. The advisors had expertise in evaluation and in the substantive areas of children's diet, physical activity, and related issues. In 2007 RWJF awarded $3 million to the Foundation of the Centers for Disease Control and Prevention for the Early Assessment initiative. Of this award, $2.4 million was devoted to screening and reviewing innovations. The remaining $600,000 was reserved to conduct a formal evaluation of the top priority identified in year one.

Three divisions of the National Center for Chronic Disease Prevention contributed staff to direct the effort: the Division of Nutrition, Physical Activity, and Obesity; the Division of Adolescent and School Health; and the Prevention Research Center Program of the Division of Adult and Community Health. ICF Macro coordinated the nomination, screening, and EA process and convened the expert panel meetings. The model has been presented twice at meetings of the American Evaluation Association, first as a planned initiative and later on the basis of the year one results. Because of feedback from prevention researchers and evaluators, and on the basis of 2 years' experience, we believe the approach to be sound.

What We Discovered About SSA From the Early Assessment Initiative

The chapters that follow give a detailed description of the Early Assessment initiative on childhood obesity prevention: the methods and overall results, the conduct of evaluability assessments, and the effects of the process on our research agenda and the field of childhood obesity prevention. In this first chapter, however, we want to reflect on the initiative as our first full implementation of the SSA Method as well as the challenges that SSA posed from an evaluation standpoint.

Selection of Priority Areas. Our first challenge lay in selecting priority areas for assessment. CDC selected these priority areas once a year, in consultation with RWJF, expert advisors, potential users, and collaborating institutions and organizations such as NIH and the U.S. Department of Agriculture (USDA). Selection of topic areas reflects the first difference between the SSA Method and the SWAT approach; SWATs are intended to be one-at-a-time assessments. The initial pool was an artifact of the funding and timing, not an essential design feature of SWAT.

The Early Assessment topics reflected a variety of priorities, such as a need to assess lesser-known areas for potential investment and the particular information needs of collaborating organizations and potential users. Cronbach (1982) addressed this challenge: the need to select evaluation topics for their ability to reduce uncertainty about social programs and to maximize leverage for social change. Our selection of the priority areas in the Early Assessment initiative reflects some of the tradeoffs in doing so. We debated whether to focus primarily on highly topical but prevalent types of innovations, such as school district local wellness policies and farmers' market interventions. We argued that choosing prevalent policy or program types would tell us about opportunities and challenges in these emerging areas of prevention. Alternatively, we could focus on finding truly unusual innovations that might constitute a potential breakthrough for childhood obesity prevention. We concluded that a mix of both prevalent and unusual innovations would ensure the most useful information. The three innovations described in Chapter 4 give a sense of the range of innovations, and two of them are potential breakthroughs.

The Nomination Process. CDC staff called for nominations of innovations in each of the 2 years. The call went to public health professionals and researchers, supplemented by existing inventories of environmental interventions maintained by CDC, RWJF, and other foundations. The challenge encountered in the nomination process was to diversify the sources for nominations. Evaluation professionals have encountered this problem in the use of snowball sampling, where the goal is to diversify the "seeds" for the growing sample, thus covering many perspectives. Even though the call for nominations was fairly broad, it addressed health professionals primarily. With time, the network for possible nominations is becoming much broader, encompassing for example, city managers and planners, parks and recreation directors, and the Grocery Manufacturers Association. Future versions of the SSA Method might consider alternative strategies to identify innovations. Some possibilities would be to deliberately expand the professional networks that might provide nominations, or to issue a challenge akin to the X Prize (http://www.xprize.org/x-prizes/overview). Another strong possibility is to employ outlier strategies to identify populations and communities where innovations may have contributed to positive changes. This approach was employed usefully in school improvement research (Teddie & Stringfield, 2007). It would be eminently feasible given the many localities that now routinely collect information on children's physical activity, dietary intake, and body mass index (Dietz, Story, & Leviton, 2009; National Center for Chronic Disease Prevention and Health Promotion, 2009).

In the area of nominations and inclusion criteria we find one of the strongest differences between the SSA Model and the SWAT initiative to which it bears such a strong resemblance. The SWAT project required that worksites had to be tracking some positive gains in obesity reduction and other health outcomes that were the focus of the SWAT project. By examining existing data collection systems at sites, the CDC team was also able to assess data access and the potential capacity for data collection essential for a rigorous evaluation. In the SSA Method, we assumed things were happening so quickly on so many fronts that we did not want to preclude potentially good ideas for lack of existing data. Moreover in the areas under study by the Early Assessment initiative, good data were unlikely to be available. Worksite data varied in quality, but at least the worksites were collecting participation data, body mass index, or other health-related measures (Dunet et al., 2008; Hersey et al., 2008).

Initial Expert Panel Review. The panel members rated each innovation independently, and then through discussion they determined which innovations warranted evaluability assessment. Thus the expert panel served as gatekeepers for progress to the later steps. This is necessary because some innovators may push to get recognition and funding for their innovations, regardless of potential merit. We employed a number of criteria throughout the process of selecting innovations. These criteria were informed by the literature on evaluation and on prevention and were refined by a group of thought leaders early in the development of the SSA Method:

- *Potential impact.* The intervention appears to have potential for impact on the social or physical environment that enables healthy diet and physical activity, and ultimately on the behaviors themselves. Potential impact is assessed on the basis of the intervention's conceptual logic and other pertinent characteristics such as intensity and duration. Estimate of impact is based on "face value," program documents, and brief expert input from funding organization staff and contractors, and other experts who know the intervention but are independent of it.
- *Innovativeness.* The intervention is new and different, or a significant variation on an existing promising intervention. Emphasis on innovativeness may be mitigated if the intervention represents a type or category of intervention that is prevalent in the field or of particular interest to CDC, RWJF, and collaborating organizations.
- *Reach to target population.* The likelihood or actual evidence that the intervention will achieve participation (and even retention and completion) by the target population. What proportion of the target population is likely to be affected by the intervention (Glasgow, Vogt, & Boles, 1999)?
- *Acceptability to stakeholders.* The potential or actual evidence that the intervention is acceptable and even attractive to pertinent collaborators, gatekeepers, and other necessary groups such as schools, businesses, government agencies, and grassroots groups.
- *Feasibility of implementation.* The likelihood that the intervention as designed can be implemented fully given the clarity of its goals, objectives, and strategies; complexity and leadership requirements; financial and other costs; and training and supervision requirements. If evidence exists regarding program implementation, then the extent to which the intervention "on paper" has been fully and faithfully implemented and the degree of difficulty in achieving implementation.
- *Feasibility of adoption.* The potential for similar sites or organizations to adopt the intervention.
- *Intervention sustainability.* The likelihood that the intervention can continue over time without special resources or extraordinary leadership.

NEW DIRECTIONS FOR EVALUATION • DOI: 10.1002/ev

- *Generalizability.* The degree to which the intervention has been or has potential to be adapted for other populations and settings.
- *Staff and organizational capacity.* Sponsoring organization and staff have the capacity to participate fully in an evaluability assessment, learn from it, and further develop the intervention.

A challenge at this stage concerned the assumptions that individual experts brought to the table. It was imperative that the experts be present and engaged in discussion of their assumptions as they applied these criteria. Not even the most accomplished experts have perfect knowledge of their substantive field, especially when it is evolving as rapidly as childhood obesity prevention. Together, however, they had enough knowledge to rule in and rule out what was likely to be effective, on the basis of the criteria. In fact, the experts were fascinated by these real-world practices.

In Chapter 5, we offer an example of how experts' assumptions changed because of their in-person interaction; initially they dismissed the idea that farmers' markets would have any power to affect diet. In the expert panel discussions, both at this stage and after the evaluability assessments, the panel had the opportunity for reality testing about new developments making it more plausible that farmers' markets would assist the goal of obesity prevention.

In the use of expert judgment, we find a second difference between the SSA Method and SWAT. SSA requires a large number of nominations precisely so that expert judges can begin to identify the high-priority innovations that plausibly have the largest effects, reach the largest portion of the affected population, and decrease uncertainty about leverage for change (Cronbach, 1982). Unlike SSA, the SWAT project did not use an initial expert review to screen nominations, moving directly to staff analysis and requests for site visits. SWAT employed outside expert judgment only after site visit reports and data were available. Nevertheless, Hersey et al. (2008) concluded that the nine worksite programs were exemplary. The SWAT procedures were probably warranted because the field already knew a lot about worksite obesity prevention and SWAT could focus its efforts without the initial expert judgment.

Evaluability Assessments. The innovations identified by the expert panel were then invited to undergo evaluability assessment. Joseph Wholey originated evaluability assessments, a method that documents "the objectives, expectations, and information needs of program managers and policy makers; explores program reality; assesses the likelihood that program activities will reach measurable progress toward program objectives; and assesses the extent to which evaluation information is likely to be used by program management" (1979, p. xiii). Evaluability assessment depends on documenting the intervention's design, developing a logic model of the intervention being assessed, consulting stakeholders who have an interest in the intervention, and documenting (often in briefest outline) implementation of the intervention. At each step in the process, the logic model is revised to reflect the reality of the intervention. A report is produced on each intervention, which assesses the plausibility of the intervention producing the outcomes and also assesses the degree to which the organization, the available data collection, and other features of the innovation make it ready for evaluation.

Later chapters present much more operational detail on how evaluability assessments were conducted in the RWJF/CDC initiative. In this chapter, we merely want to contrast the usual practice of conducting evaluability assessments with how they were conducted in the context of the SSA. We see two major differences.

1. *Standalone versus multiple assessments.* In the literature on evaluability assessments, the presumption is that a single policy or program is assessed. In the SSA Method, 48 assessments of innovations sharing common themes were undertaken. Several published evaluability assessments do include multiple sites or states, but they do so in order to assess state or local implementation and stakeholder viewpoints about a single program, not to explore innovative approaches to solve a common problem (e.g., Mulkern, 2005).
2. *Decision rule for continuing to full evaluation.* Although the information from evaluability assessments generally has been found to be useful, often it does not result in further evaluation (Rog, 1985). Two likely reasons are that program logic models may not be consistent with resources and activities, and that the logic models themselves may not be plausible to achieve program outcomes. For the SSA Method, it is to be expected that only a modest number of interventions would merit subsequent evaluation; in fact, the approach takes advantage of this tendency. SSA depends on the evaluability assessments to winnow through interventions that may have such problems and identify those diamonds in the rough that merit further evaluation.

A challenge at this stage was to make clear to all stakeholders that evaluability assessment is not the same as evaluation. EAs are a preevaluation activity, designed to maximize the chances that any subsequent evaluation will result in useful information. Another challenge was that resources did not permit an extensive process of information gathering and revision of logic models. A single site visit was supplemented by many phone calls— yet in reality, the process had to be curtailed in comparison to other evaluability assessments we have read about and conducted ourselves.

Expert Panel Review of Evaluability Assessments. The expert panel reconvened to review the reports from the evaluability assessments and rate each intervention, for both its promise to prevent childhood obesity and its readiness for evaluation. Ratings focused on the degree of promise and readiness, not a yes-or-no decision about promise. This gave a more nuanced picture of each intervention and encourage further development, improvements, and constructive feedback to the developers and managers of the interventions.

Again the expert panels served as gatekeepers, but this time their role was to assure that the nine criteria listed in step 3 (potential effectiveness, innovativeness, reach, and so on) were applied in these ratings. Using these criteria, with the expert panel as gatekeepers, ensures that the project can resist any outside pressures to pronounce certain interventions as promising before a formal evaluation is available. In several federal settings, expert panels such as these have been effective in ensuring that only the evidence-based programs are endorsed by the government for dissemination (Centers for Disease Control and Prevention, 2008; Katzenmeyer & Haertel, 1986).

The expert panel deliberations were interesting at this phase because the evaluability assessments constituted a further reality test of the panel's assumptions about the way that environment and policy would affect children's diet and physical activity. Indeed, as Chapter 5 describes further, the panel had to be restrained from developing entire research programs around some of the innovations presented. The process was helpful not only for identifying the innovations worth testing but also for the range of ideas about constructive evaluation questions and the designs to study these questions.

In some cases the panel was able to review several examples of a similar innovation, as in the case of school wellness policies for low-income districts and farmers' markets for inner-city communities. The panel proposed a cluster evaluation for the farmers' markets, for which CDC has now authorized funding. Further, the discussions offered the possibility of developing new innovation "types." By this we mean several exemplars gave rise to an abstract model that included several essential program components. It will be instructive in the future to see whether the idea of an innovation type assists the process of evaluation and later translation back to practice.

Use of Information. Three distinct uses of information have resulted from the SSA Method as applied to childhood obesity prevention. First and foremost, we have identified several outstanding innovations that are worthy of support for more rigorous evaluation. Other innovations were deemed promising and ready for evaluation. For this secondary group, the goal is to assist them and their research partners in applying for development and evaluation support, from foundations or the federal government.

The intended evaluation projects that follow from the SSA Method are fundamentally different from those intended by the SWAT initiative. SWAT assumes that the innovating organizations will carry out their own evaluations with technical assistance to increase their internal evaluation capacity. The SWAT focus on internal evaluation is consistent with CDC's public health partnership with state and local health departments. The worksite programs studied by SWAT might decide to undertake internal evaluations, and the results might offer valuable information to the field. They might, but we note that researchers have been largely responsible for the body of evidence on worksite obesity prevention (Katz et al., 2005).

In contrast, the SSA Method assumes that the next step is rigorous evaluation of the highest-priority innovations, not self-evaluation of all promising innovations. For the policy and environmental innovations studied through the SSA Method in the Early Assessment initiative, we assumed that research expertise, not internal evaluation, was absolutely essential to conducting follow-on evaluation. The challenges of measuring environmental changes to prevent children's overweight were simply too new and formidable for non-researchers to address by themselves (Ohri Vachaspati & Leviton, in press; Story et al., 2009). Follow-on evaluation resources must go to organizations with substantial expertise in measurement, sampling, design, high-quality data collection, and analysis.

A second major use of the findings from the Early Assessment initiative and the SSA Method was the constructive feedback given to 48 intervention developers and technical assistance so they could improve their efforts. The evaluability assessments and the second expert review are excellent vehicles for program development. Yet the program development that results from evaluability assessment does not receive much attention in the literature (Leviton et al., in press; Smith, 1989). The intervention developers and managers genuinely appreciated CDC technical assistance and found it useful (see Chapter 5). To achieve this, CDC staff oversaw the feedback process and gave access to content experts to further advise the innovation developers on program improvement. This type of use also demonstrates differences between SWAT and the SSA Method. SWAT extends technical assistance for program development and building the innovators' own evaluation capacity, while the SSA Method offers it for program development only.

The third use of information was for cross site synthesis. The syntheses were developed from several sources: the available literature on these topics, the evaluability assessments (for emerging themes), and the discussions of the expert panel. A surprise in this process was that all the innovations were informative, whether they passed the test for promise, or not! Indeed, it was helpful to be able to discuss fatal flaws in the logic or activities, because this helped to articulate some of the critically important features of similar innovations. Indeed, one of the syntheses is being used as the basis of published CDC guidance on development of comprehensive school physical activity programs (Pitt Barnes et al., 2009a). Even though none of the innovations on this topic met the highest standard of promise and readiness for evaluation, the EAs furnished many insights for CDC guidance on how to improve program operation.

Cross-site use of findings was similar in some ways to the experience of the SWAT initiative. The data that worksites collected in the SWAT initiative were helpful to decrease uncertainty about effective practices in any worksite obesity prevention program. In the same way, synthesis of cross-site learning from the Early Assessment initiative informed decision makers about program elements that would plausibly increase the effectiveness of policy and environmental changes to prevent childhood obesity.

In another sense, however, the cross-site syntheses of the Early Assessment initiative differed radically from the SWAT synthesis for worksite obesity prevention. The SWAT approach is intended as a middle ground between rigorous study of outcomes and the connoisseurship model of evaluation that uses expert judgment only (Dunet et al., 2008). For worksite programs this middle ground is defensible, but it is not defensible for most of the innovations identified by the SSA Method in the Early Assessment initiative. Good studies have already been conducted on the effectiveness of obesity prevention and treatment in worksites (Katz et al., 2005). This permits elaboration of components or practices that could optimize the effects of worksite programs and allows SWAT to take a defensible middle ground in recommending those practices for wider adoption. Unlike the worksite setting, tests of effectiveness have not been conducted for the policy and environmental changes examined by the SSA Method in the Early Assessment initiative. Therefore we need to be exceedingly cautious in fully testing their effectiveness before recommending adoption by others.

Conclusions

We conclude that the Systematic Screening and Assessment Method offers a cost-effective strategy to ensure more productive and useful evaluations. The Early Assessment initiative represents proof of concept for the step-by-step screening process, which clearly sharpened the focus for evaluation at every step. We acknowledge that no evaluability assessments were conducted for the nominations that were eliminated by the expert panel, so we cannot compare the potential yield from those that were screened out. As described in Chapters 2 and 3, however, it is implausible that they would have been deemed promising or ready for evaluation—barring any new information that the evaluability assessments might have revealed. The same expert panelists who dismissed them in the first review would have dismissed them again in the second review, using the very same criteria.

One might argue that truly powerful innovations might have been identified for evaluation without SSA. The New York City day care regulations and the Philadelphia Fresh Food Financing Initiative are described in Chapter 4. Both of these innovations were fairly well known to the field of childhood obesity prevention, or could easily have become so. Yet for every innovation that passed the screening and assessment stages, there were several that were well known and did not pass. In any case, the evaluability assessment process assisted in formulating evaluation plans, and indeed, programs of evaluation inquiry about the innovations.

Some of our expert panelists were dismayed at how few innovations seemed truly potent to achieve impact, even in the group of 20 that were finally identified. Does a school policy really contribute to a reversal of the childhood obesity epidemic? Does a new supermarket in a "food desert" do this for poor populations, who are most at risk of obesity? Readers will need to judge this for themselves. Certainly, two of the innovations described as case studies in Chapter 4 are very plausible and seem powerful enough to achieve such impact. Also, it is clear that no single policy or environmental change will produce the impact that is needed; these are cumulative changes that only together may prevent childhood obesity (Leviton, 2008).

References

Agency for Healthcare Research and Quality. (2002). What is AHRQ? Retrieved April 25, 2009, from http://www.ahrq.gov/about/whatis.htm

Berwick, D. (2003). Disseminating innovation in health care. *Journal of the American Medical Association, 289*,1969–1975.

Campbell, D. T. (1977). Descriptive epistemology: Psychological, sociological, and evolutionary. William James Lectures, Harvard University.

Carman, J. G., & Fredericks, K. A. (2008). Nonprofits and evaluation: Empirical evidence from the field. In J. G. Carman & K. A. Fredericks (Eds.), *Nonprofits and evaluation. New Directions for Evaluation, 119*, 51–72.

Centers for Disease Control and Prevention. (2008). *Replicating effective programs plus.* Retrieved April 25, 2009, from http://www.cdc.gov/hiv/topics/prev_prog/rep/index.htm

Cheung, K., Dawkins, N., Kettel Khan, L., & Leviton, L. C. (2009). *Early Assessment of Programs and Policies to Prevent Childhood Obesity: Synthesis of initiatives that increase access to healthy foods.* Atlanta: U.S. Department of Health and Human Services, Centers for Disease Control and Prevention.

Cook, T. D., Leviton, L. C., & Shadish, W. R. (1985). Evaluation research. In G. Lindzey & E. Aronson (Eds.), *The handbook of social psychology* (3rd ed., pp. 699–777). New York: Random House.

Cronbach, L. J. (1982). *Designing evaluations of education and social programs.* San Francisco: Jossey-Bass.

Davis, H. R., & Salasin, S. E. (1975). The utilization of evaluation. In E. L. Struening & M. Guttentag (Eds.), *Handbook of evaluation research.* Thousand Oaks, CA: Sage.

Dietz, B., Story, M., & Leviton, L. C. (Eds.). (2009). Issues and implications of screening, surveillance, and reporting of children's body mass index. *Pediatrics*, Supplement 2008–3586.

Dunet, D. O., Sparling, P. B., Hersey, J., Williams-Pierhota, P., Hill, M. D., Hanssen, C., et al. (2008). A new evaluation tool to obtain practice-based evidence in worksite health promotion programs. *Preventing Chronic Disease, 5*(4). Retrieved September 25, 2009, from http://www.cdc.gov/pcd/issues/2008/oct/07_0173.htm

Emshoff, J. G., Blakely, C., Gottschalk, R., Mayer, J., Davidson, W. S., & Erickson, S. (1987). Innovation in education and criminal justice: Measuring fidelity of implementation and program effectiveness. *Educational Evaluation and Policy Analysis, 9*(4), 300–311.

Glasgow, R. E., Green, L. W., Klesges, L. W., Abrams, D. B., Fisher, E. B., Goldstein, M. B., et al. (2006). External validity: We need to do more. *Annals of Behavioral Medicine, 3*, 12.

Glasgow, R. E., Vogt, T. M., & Boles, S. M. (1999). Evaluating the public health impact of health promotion interventions: The RE-AIM framework. *American Journal of Public Health, 89*, 1323–1327.

Griffin, S. F., Wilcox, S., Ory, M. G., Lattimore, D., Leviton, L. C., Castro, C. M., et al. (2009). Results from the Active for Life Process Evaluation: Program delivery and fidelity. *Health Education Research, 24*(3). Retrieved September 25, 2009, from http://her.oxfordjournals.org/cgi/content/full/cyp017v1?ijkey=5PCzlpzauEWy1W8&keytype=ref

Henry, G. T. (2003). Influential evaluations. *American Journal of Evaluation, 24*, 515–524.

Hersey, J., Williams-Peihota, P., Sparling, P. B., Alexander, J., Hill, M. D., Isenberg, K. B., et al. (2008). Promising practices in promotion of healthy weight at small and medium-sized U.S. worksites. *Prevention of Chronic Disease, 5*(4), A122.

Katz, D. L., O'Connell, M., Yeh, M. C., Nawaz, H., Njike, V., Anderson, L. M., et al. (2005). Public health strategies for preventing and controlling overweight and obesity in school and worksite settings: A report on recommendations of the Task Force on Community Preventive Services (*MMWR* Recommendation Report, 54(RR-10)),. Atlanta: Centers for Disease Control and Prevention.

Katzenmeyer, C. G., & Haertel, G. (1986, April). *Analyzing the JDRP as an evaluation process.* Paper presented at the Annual Meeting of the American Educational Research Association, San Francisco. ERIC Number ED276746.

Koplan, J. P., Liverman, C. T., & Kraak, V. I. (Eds.). (2001). *Preventing childhood obesity: Health in the balance.* Washington, DC: National Academies Press.

Leviton, L. C. (2008). Children's healthy weight and the school environment. *Annals of the American Academy of Political and Social Science, 615,* 38–55.

Leviton, L. C., Collins, C., Laird, B., & Kratt, P. (1998). Teaching evaluation using evaluability assessment. *Evaluation, 4*(4), 389–409.

Leviton, L. C., & Guinan, M. E. (2003). Contributions of HIV prevention evaluation to public health program evaluation. In R. O. Valdiserri (Ed.), *Dawning answers: How the HIV/AIDS epidemic has helped to strengthen public health* (pp. 155–176). New York: Oxford University Press.

Leviton, L. C., Kettel-Khan, L., Rog, D., Dawkins, N., & Cotton, D. (in press). Evaluability assessment to improve public health. In *Annual Review of Public Health, Vol. 31.*

Lipsey, M. W. (1988). Practice and malpractice in evaluation research. *Evaluation Practice, 9*(4), 5–25.

Mulkern, V. (2005, October). *Evaluability assessment of the Mental Health Block Grant Program.* Presented at the annual meeting of the American Evaluation Association, Toronto.

National Center for Chronic Disease Prevention and Health Promotion, Division of Adolescent and School Health. (2009). *YRBSS: Youth Risk Behavior Surveillance System.* Retrieved September 29, 2009, from http://www.cdc.gov/HealthyYouth/yrbs/index.htm

National Institute of Justice. (2008). *Strategic goals: Creating relevant knowledge and tools.* Retrieved April 25, 2009, from http://www.ojp.usdoj.gov/nij/about/strategic-goals.htm

National Institute of Mental Health. (2009). *The National Institute of Mental Health Strategic Plan.* Retrieved April 25, 2009, from http://www.nimh.nih.gov/about/strategic-planning-reports/index.shtml

National Institutes of Health. (2008). *Re-engineering the Clinical Research Enterprise: Translational Research.* Retrieved April 25, 2009, from http://nihroadmap.nih.gov/clinicalresearch/overview-translational.asp

Ohri Vachaspati, P., & Leviton, L. C. (in press). Measuring food environments: A guide to available instruments. *American Journal of Health Promotion.*

OMG Center for Collaborative Learning. (2007). *Brief assessments of community-based childhood obesity prevention within the Injury Free Coalition for Kids initiative sites: Final report.* Philadelphia: Author.

Pitt Barnes, S., Robin, L., Dawkins, N., Leviton, L., & Kettel-Khan, L. (2009a). *Early Assessment of Programs and Policies to Prevent Childhood Obesity Evaluability Assessment Synthesis Report: Comprehensive school physical activity programs.* Atlanta: U.S. Department of Health and Human Services, Centers for Disease Control and Prevention.

Pitt Barnes, S., Robin, L., Dawkins, N., Leviton, L., & Kettel-Khan, L. (2009b). *Early Assessment of Programs and Policies to Prevent Childhood Obesity Evaluability Assessment Synthesis Report: Local wellness policy.* Atlanta: U.S. Department of Health and Human Services, Centers for Disease Control and Prevention.

Reichert, C. S. (1994). Summative evaluation, formative evaluation, and tactical research. *Evaluation Practice, 15*(3), 275–281.

Rhodes, S. (2007). *Experiences with exploratory evaluation: A summary of lessons learned from twelve exploratory evaluations.* Winston-Salem, NC: Wake Forest University.

Rog, D. J. (1985). *A methodological analysis of evaluability assessment.* Unpublished doctoral dissertation, Vanderbilt University.

Rog, D., & Gutman, M. (2007). Brief assessments of environmental and policy interventions on healthy eating: Lessons emerging about the methodology. Princeton, NJ: Gutman Associates.

Rossi, P. H., Lipsey, M. W., & Freeman, H. E. (2003). *Evaluation: A systematic approach.* Thousand Oaks, CA: Sage.

Schlotthauer, A. E., Badler, A., Cook, S. C., Perez, D. J., & Chin, M. H. (2008). Evaluating interventions to reduce health care disparities: An RWJF program. *Health Affairs, 27*(2), 568–573.

Shadish, W. R., Cook, T. D., & Leviton, L. C. (1991). *Foundations of program evaluation: Theorists and their theories.* Thousand Oaks, CA: Sage.

Skelton, S., Dawkins, N., Leviton, L., & Kettel Khan, L. (2009). *Early Assessment of Programs and Policies to Prevent Childhood Obesity evaluability assessment synthesis brief: Built environment and land use programs.* Atlanta: U.S. Department of Health and Human Services, Centers for Disease Control and Prevention.

Smith, M. F. (1989). *Evaluability assessment: A practical approach.* Boston: Kluwer Academic.

Story, M., Giles-Corti, B., Yaroch, A. L., Cummins, S., Frank, L. D., Huang, T.T.-K., et al. (2009). Work Group IV: Future directions for measures of the food and physical activity environments. *American Journal of Preventive Medicine, 36*(4S), S182–S188.

Substance Abuse and Mental Health Services Administration. (2009). NREPP: SAMHSA's National Registry of Evidence-based Programs and Practices. Retrieved April 25, 2009, from http://www.nrepp.samhsa.gov/index.asp

Teddie, C., & Stringfield, S. (2007). The history of the school effectiveness and improvement research in the USA focusing on the past quarter century. In T. Townsend (Ed.), *International handbook of school effectiveness and improvement: Review, reflection and reframing* (pp. 131–166). Dordrecht, Netherlands: Springer.

U.S. Department of Education. What Works Clearinghouse. Retrieved April 25, 2009, from http://ies.ed.gov/ncee/wwc/

Weiss, C. H. (1987). Evaluating social programs. What have we learned? *Society, 25*(1), 40–45.

Wethington, H., Kirkconnell Hall, M., Dawkins, N., Leviton, L., & Kettel Khan, L. (2009). *Early Assessment of Programs and Policies to Prevent Childhood Obesity Evaluability Assessment Synthesis Report: Childcare initiatives in afterschool and daycare settings.* Atlanta: U.S. Department of Health and Human Services, Centers for Disease Control and Prevention.

Wholey, J. S. (1979) *Evaluation: Promise and performance.* Washington, DC: Urban Institute.

Wholey, J. S. (2004). Assessing the feasibility and likely usefulness of evaluation. In J. S. Wholey, H. P. Hatry, & K. E. Newcomer (Eds.), *Handbook of practical program evaluation.* San Francisco: Jossey-Bass.

Wilson, D. B., & Lipsey, M. W. (2001). The role of method in treatment effectiveness research: Evidence from meta-analysis. *Psychological Methods, 6,* 413–429.

LAURA C. LEVITON is the coauthor of Foundations of Program Evaluation *and is currently Special Advisor for Evaluation at the Robert Wood Johnson Foundation, where for the past 10 years she has overseen more than 80 evaluations at the national, state, and local levels.*

MARJORIE A. GUTMAN is the Principal of Gutman Research Associates, with 25 years' experience in program evaluation and development to address public health and behavioral health challenges.

Dawkins, N., Wethington, H., Kettel Khan, L., Grunbaum, J. A., Robin, L., Pitt Barnes, S., et al. (2010). Applying the Systematic Screening and Assessment Method to childhood obesity prevention. In L. C. Leviton, L. Kettel Khan, & N. Dawkins (Eds.), *The Systematic Screening and Assessment Method: Finding innovations worth evaluating. New Directions for Evaluation,* 125, 33–49.

2

Applying the Systematic Screening and Assessment Method to Childhood Obesity Prevention

Nicola Dawkins, Holly Wethington, Laura Kettel Khan,
Jo Anne Grunbaum, Leah Robin, Seraphine Pitt Barnes,
David Cotton, Diane O. Dunet, Laura C. Leviton

Abstract

The authors describe application of the Systematic Screening and Assessment (SSA) Method to an initiative called the Early Assessment of Programs and Policies to Prevent Childhood Obesity. Over a 2-year period, a national network of practitioners, policy makers, and funders nominated programs and policies across five substantive areas: school district local wellness policies, school-based comprehensive physical activity programs, day care and after-school programs, access to healthy foods in low-income communities, and changes in the built environment to promote physical activity. The role of an expert panel in selecting innovations for evaluability assessment on the basis of the likelihood for a positive health impact is described. © Wiley Periodicals, Inc., and the American Evaluation Association.

Note: The findings and conclusions presented are those of the authors and do not necessarily represent the official position of the agencies.

NEW DIRECTIONS FOR EVALUATION, no. 125, Spring 2010 © Wiley Periodicals, Inc., and the American Evaluation Association. Published online in Wiley InterScience (www.interscience.wiley.com) • DOI: 10.1002/ev.319

The Early Assessment of Programs and Policies to Prevent Childhood Obesity initiative began in 2007 as a 2-year project to identify and assess community-level programs and policies that held promise of preventing childhood obesity. The rates of childhood obesity and overweight have increased significantly over the last decade (Ogden et al., 2006), but there is limited scientific evidence about effective obesity prevention (Koplan, Liverman, & Kraak, 2001). To reduce the prevalence of children's obesity, changes are needed both to decrease their calorie intake and to increase their daily physical activity (Wang, Gortmaker, Sobol, & Kuntz, 2006). The Guide to Community Preventive Services presents environmental and policy approaches (Guide to Community Preventive Services, 2009), and the Institute of Medicine recommended using policy and environmental changes, as well as more conventional health education, to sustain behavioral changes and reach a large proportion of children at risk (Koplan et al., 2001). Following this recommendation, the Early Assessment initiative focused on identifying promising policies and programming, i.e., innovations, that affect children's food and physical activity environment.

The current large scale of programmatic activity related to the childhood obesity problem, coupled with the limited evidence base regarding what is effective, constituted an opportunity to apply the Systematic Screening and Assessment (SSA) Method to identify and assess practice-based innovations. The method pairs identification of potentially promising innovations (in this case addressing childhood obesity prevention) with appraisal through evaluability assessment. This chapter details application of the SSA Method in the Early Assessment initiative (see Table 2.1).

Steps in the Systematic Screening and Assessment Method

Both the method and the results are presented for each of the six steps in the process, followed by discussion of this application of the SSA Method.

Step 1: Selection of Priority Topics for Assessment. A first step in the SSA Method is determining the topics for assessment. When possible, these priority topics should be selected in conjunction with key stakeholders and potential users.

Stakeholder Consultation. The Early Assessment initiative project team created a Funders Advisory Committee comprising representatives of organizations that support national programs and policies to address childhood obesity. The committee included staff from the Centers for Disease Control and Prevention (CDC), the U.S. Department of Agriculture (USDA), the National Institutes of Health (NIH), and the Robert Wood Johnson Foundation (RWJF). In addition, the committee included members from the Healthy Eating Active Living Convergence Partnership, a collaborative group of nonprofit organizations and private foundations.

NEW DIRECTIONS FOR EVALUATION • DOI: 10.1002/ev

Table 2.1. Steps in the Systematic Screening and Assessment Method

Step	General Details on Application
1. Selection of priority topics for assessment	Identify funders to consider issues of greatest importance to be explored
2. Request for nominations and application of inclusion criteria	Cast a wide net for requesting nominations Search for novel innovations Review nominations against inclusion and exclusion criteria
3. Expert panel review and selection of innovations for evaluability assessment	Summarize innovations for expert panel Conduct blind ratings Convene panelists to discuss and rerate each remaining nomination Finalize list of innovations to undergo EA
4. Engaging a distributed network to conduct evaluability assessments	Select and train appropriate staff for EA teams Conduct EAs Develop EA reports
5. Second expert panel review	Summarize EA reports Conduct blind ratings Convene panelists to determine potential impact and readiness for outcomes-focused evaluation
6. Use of information	Position the most promising innovations for rigorous evaluation Provide constructive feedback to all innovations for further refinement Synthesize what is known about these innovations and evaluation issues that emerge

The committee served three functions. Initially, they suggested topic areas on which the Early Assessment initiative should focus. Once findings were available from the initiative, the committee members were asked to provide technical assistance and development support for programs with good ideas that were neither fully developed nor ready for an outcomes-focused evaluation. In addition, they were asked to consider funding to evaluate the programs and policies judged to be both promising and ready for outcomes-focused evaluation.

Topic Areas for Screening and Assessment. Topic areas selected as priorities in year one were (1) child care programs and policies in after-school or day care settings (AS/DC; Story, Kaphingst, & French, 2006), (2) implementation of School District Local Wellness Policies (LWP; Child Nutrition and WIC Reauthorization Act of 2004; Wechsler, McKenna, Lee, & Deitz,

2004), and (3) programs and policies that increase access to healthier foods in low-income, inner-city communities ("food access"; Story, Kaphingst, Robinson-O'Brien, & Glanz, 2008).

In year two, the topics were modified and expanded to include (1) AS/DC programs and policies with more stringent physical activity and nutrition requirements; (2) food access programs and policies with an emphasis on supermarket, convenience store, and restaurant interventions; (3) school-based comprehensive school physical activity programs (CSPA), which encompass programming before, during, and after the school day (National Association for Sport and Physical Education, 2008); and (4) land use and built environment and transportation projects and policies ("built environment") (Heath et al., 2006).

Step 2: Request for Nominations and Application of Inclusion Criteria. In both years of the Early Assessment initiative, program and policy solicitation began by distributing a nomination form through chronic disease prevention listservs. Listserv subscribers then solicited input from their colleagues, who were the originators of many of the innovations, such that nominations were obtained from school district administrators, city managers, food systems experts, extension service professionals, and other diverse sources not usually reached by public health practitioners. In addition, the project team contacted more than 25 national and regional organizations that work on issues of childhood obesity prevention and asked them to distribute the nomination form to their contacts.

In Table 2.2 we present the yield from the nominations process by year and by topic area. In year one, the nomination period lasted 2 months and yielded 282 programs and policies across the three topic areas. In year two, after 3 months, there were only 97 innovations nominated across the after-school and day care, food access, and CSPA topic areas. Because of the smaller number of nominated innovations, the Early Assessment initiative project team continued to solicit nominations for another 3 months. In addition, the project team was concerned that the initiative had reached saturation for appropriate innovations in the initial three topic areas of year two. The project team therefore added a fourth topic area: built environment innovations. After 6 months, the project team received nominations of 176 total innovations for review.

Not all the nominated innovations were appropriate for review, however, and the initiative project team developed and applied inclusion and exclusion criteria for each topic area to screen the nominations systematically. The criteria ensured the nominated programs and policies were (1) environmental or policy interventions (those involving a change to the environment or in relevant policy, rather than solely seeking direct changes in individual behavior), (2) suitable for implementation in the United States, (3) already developed and implemented sufficiently so that an evaluability assessment could study their operation, (4) located in appropriate settings (e.g., low-income, addressing higher-risk populations), (5) targeting children ages 3 to 17, (6)

Table 2.2. Yield of the Nominations Process by Year and Topic Area

	Nominated	Met Criteria	Summarized
Year one			
AS/DC	81	34	25
LWP	146	58	25
Food Access	55	23	22
Year one total	282	115 (41%)	72 (26%)
Year two			
AS/DC	86	27	24
CSPA	39	7	7
Food Access	29	11	11
Built Environment	22	14	14
Year two total	176	59 (34%)	56 (32%)
Total years one and two	458	174 (38%)	128 (28%)

Note: Percentages indicate the proportion of nominations received that met criteria and were then summarized. AS/DC = after-school and day care innovations; LWP = school district local wellness policies; CSPA = comprehensive school physical activity innovations.

not previously or currently the subject of outcomes-focused evaluation, and (7) not strict replications of evidence-based models (although adaptations of such models were included). In addition, where appropriate we established specific criteria for various topic areas. For example, in the after-school and day care topic area we sought innovations where improving nutrition or physical activity for children was the primary goal, not a subsidiary one.

The project team reviewed each nominated program or policy against the inclusion and exclusion criteria and contacted the nominators for clarification and additional information as needed. For programs and policies that met the inclusion criteria, the initiative project team developed brief summaries of most innovations.

In year one, 115 (41%) of the nominated innovations met the inclusion criteria, and 72 (26%) were summarized for review by the expert panel. In year two, 59 (34%) of the nominated innovations met the inclusion criteria, and 56 (32%) were summarized. Across both years, 458 policies and programs were nominated, 174 (38%) met our criteria, and 128 (28%) were summarized for the expert panel. The 46 innovations that were not summarized included cases where the program contact could not be reached, nominations were received after the deadline, the nominating institution nominated more than one program for consideration, or there were already multiple innovations summarized from that city or state. In the latter two instances, a single program or policy was selected that appeared strongest on the basis of the nominations. Most nominations came from the LWP and AS/DC topic areas (and, in year two, CSPA); however, only a small percentage of them met our inclusion criteria.

NEW DIRECTIONS FOR EVALUATION • DOI: 10.1002/ev

Early Assessment project team members used a standard template to develop a two-page summary about each program or policy, including the specific criteria expert panel members were asked to consider in rating each innovation. The criteria are potential impact, innovativeness, reach to target population, acceptability to stakeholders, feasibility of implementation, feasibility of adoption, intervention sustainability, generalizability, and staff and organizational capacity (see Chapter 1 for details).

Step 3: Expert Panel Review and Selection of Innovations for Evaluability Assessment. The project team established a 15-member expert panel to review and select innovations to undergo evaluability assessments and to determine from the results of the assessments those innovations ready for outcomes-focused evaluation with the greatest potential for positive health impact. The panel members were nationally recognized experts who have published in peer-reviewed journals in their respective areas of expertise, including evaluation, measurement of environmental innovations and health outcomes, nutrition, physical activity, school-aged youth, and community programs.

In Table 2.3 we present the yield from steps 3 through 5: initial selection of innovations, evaluability assessments conducted, innovations considered potentially ready for outcomes-focused evaluation after internal review, and expert panel determinations of innovations that have high potential for positive health impact and that are ready for outcomes-focused evaluation.

Expert Panel Blind Reviews. The expert panel members reviewed two-page summaries of each innovation, blinded to the innovations' names and locations. In year one each expert panel member was assigned to review between seven and nine innovations within each topic area, ensuring that the innovation was rated by at least three expert panel members. Expert panel members completed their ratings prior to each meeting using Zoomerang, an online survey tool. Panel members had 2 weeks to review project summaries and complete their ratings. They were divided into two groups according to area of expertise to supply the ratings. One group reviewed AS/DC innovations, and the other reviewed food access innovations. At a later time, all the panel members reviewed and rated the LWP innovations, delayed to give the initiative project team time to reach contacts for the large number of nominees and apply the inclusion and exclusion criteria.

In year two, the Early Assessment initiative project team used the same rating process with the expert panel in advance of two separate meetings. Before both of the year two meetings, each expert panel member rated five or six innovations, ensuring each innovation was rated by three expert panel members.

Meetings to Select Innovations for Evaluability Assessment. In year one, panel members had one in-person meeting to discuss AS/DC and food access innovations. Later, they discussed LWP innovations during a conference call.

Table 2.3. Initiatives Selected for Evaluability Assessment and Considered Potentially Ready for Outcomes-Focused Evaluation by Year and Topic Area

	Expert Panel Selected for EA	EAs Conducted	Selected as Ready for Outcome Evaluation	Expert Panel Rated High Potential Impact and Ready for Outcome Evaluation
Year one				
AS/DC	10	10	6	2
LWP	6	6	4	3
Food Access	10	9	6	4
Year one total	26	25	16	9
Year two				
AS/DC	12	12	9	6
CSPA	2	2	1	0
Food Access	9	7	5	3
Built Environment	4	2	2	2
Year two total	27	23	17	11
Total years one and two	53	48	33	20

Note: AS/DC = after-school and day care initiatives; LWP = school district local wellness policies; CSPA = comprehensive school physical activity innovations.

In year two, there also were two separate meetings; during the meetings, the panel members discussed what they considered the most important attributes, which often involved reach of the innovation, number of sites included, and whether the innovation had both nutrition and physical activity components or otherwise appeared sufficiently comprehensive to suggest high potential for positive health impact.

The panel members selected those programs and policies they considered worthy of additional review through an evaluability assessment. After the panel's preliminary selections, the project team revealed the program and policy identities and locations, and the expert panel discussions continued with this information in mind. As seen in Table 2.3, by the end of the year one in-person meeting, the panel members had selected 20 innovations in the AS/DC and food access areas. Following a similar process during the later conference call, the panel members selected 6 LWPs for evaluability assessment visits.

In year two, the project team used a similar process, and panel members participated in two separate meetings to select innovations. The panel members selected additional AS/DC, food access, and built environment innovations. As seen in Table 2.3, in year two the expert panel selected a total of 27 innovations for evaluability assessments.

Step 4: Engaging a Distributed Network to Conduct Evaluability Assessments. For each innovation selected by the expert panel in the SSA

Method, an evaluability assessment (EA) is conducted. Using a distributed network to conduct EAs for this initiative enabled the conduct of multiple assessments in a short period of time and broadened professional experience with the evaluability assessment method.

Evaluability Assessments. At the core of the project and of the SSA Method is the evaluability assessment method (Leviton, Kettel Khan, Rog, Dawkins, & Cotton, in press; Wholey 1979, 2004). Evaluability assessment (EA) determines if an innovation is ready for an outcomes-focused evaluation, or what other evaluative activity might be most appropriate. Evaluability assessments explore an innovation's logic and design and consider likely evaluation questions, available data sources, options for data collection, and potential evaluation approaches. In the SSA Method, an EA report for each innovation discusses the plausibility of the innovation producing the intended outcomes and also assesses the degree to which the organization, the available data collection, and other features of the innovation make it ready for outcome evaluation.

EA Team Selection and Training. In both years, the project team drew on its professional network to identify a cadre of trained public health and evaluation researchers and practitioners to serve on EA teams. The project team developed and conducted a 2-day, in-person training for the EA teams. In year one, the project team trained 32 individuals, and it trained or retrained 34 in year two, for a total of 40.

Conducting Evaluability Assessments. In both years of the project, the EAs were arranged and carried out in the same manner. Teams of two people conducted each evaluability assessment. To the extent possible, assignments matched the EA team members' areas of expertise with the innovations undergoing EA. Another consideration was each person's availability to conduct the 2- to 3-day assessment visits and carry out the post-site-visit work of preparing the required summary reports. The lead EA team members estimated the average total time required for each visit at 80 work hours, including background preparation and scheduling, conducting site visits, and postsite-visit reporting.

Prior to the onsite visit, the project team obtained background documents from the contact person for each innovation and shared these materials with the assigned EA teams. The EA teams drafted logic models based on those documents to graphically describe a program or policy's activities and desired outcomes.

The Early Assessment project staff also worked closely with the contact person from each innovation to identify potential interviewees and schedule the site visit. During this time, five innovations (one in year one, four in year two) decided they were not quite far enough along in implementation or they did not have the staff capacity to make an EA visit worthwhile. As a result, the project staff coordinated 48 site visits. The project staff furnished a template to the site contact that included guidance describing the types of individuals we wished to interview. After the site contact made his or her initial recommendations of interviewees, the initiative project team and EA teams reviewed the suggested interviewees with the contact person by phone and, if needed, made additional recommendations of what kind of people it might be helpful to interview. Once the list of interviewees was agreed on, the site contact worked with those individuals to schedule their interviews.

During the site visit, the EA teams observed the surroundings of the innovation venue and conducted interviews with program or policy representatives, such as administrators, supervisors, staff, partners, and representatives of the target audience. The interviews assessed factors critical to understanding each innovation's design, current implementation, and options for evaluation, in particular the program or policy description, logic model, staffing, funding, sustainability, and existing and potential data collection activities.

Evaluability Assessment Reports. EA reports serve a critical function for the SSA Method. They are a primary source of feedback to the participating developers and managers of these innovations, and they are the basis for expert panel review to determine the promise and readiness for outcomes-focused evaluation. EA teams wrote separate reports to address each of these audiences. Internal reports, developed for the initiative project team and expert panel, described the essential components of each innovation and captured the EA teams' candid impressions of the innovations with regard to generalizability, likely impact, implications for evaluation, and related issues. External reports, developed to be shared with the developers and managers of each innovation, elaborated details on the program or policy context and findings from the EA, including recommendations for improvements in the program or policy design, its implementation, and how the innovators could prepare for evaluation.

Step 5: The Second Expert Panel Review. A second review of the visited innovations by the expert panel used the evaluability assessment reports to further reduce uncertainty about their promise, feasibility, and readiness for more rigorous evaluation. Because of the large number of innovations visited, to reduce burden on the expert panel, the project team first conducted an internal review of the reports, identified those clearly not ready for outcomes-focused evaluation, and presented the remainder to the expert panel for review.

Internal Review of EA Reports. The Early Assessment project team reviewed the EA reports and identified those innovations clearly not ready for outcomes-focused evaluation ($n = 15$ across the 2 years). Innovations were deemed not ready for evaluation for a number of reasons: (1) administrators were resistant to data collection ($n = 2$); (2) the innovation's true focus was outside the focus on physical activity and nutrition ($n = 5$); (3) the innovation had limited potential for impact because of its meager reach ($n = 2$); or (4) implementation was in the early stages, so the innovation was not appropriate for an outcomes-focused evaluation ($n = 6$). As seen in Table 2.3, the project team identified 16 innovations in year one and 17 in year two as potentially ready for outcomes-focused evaluation and presented them to the expert panel for review.

Expert Panel Blind Review. Prior to the second expert panel review meeting, the project team gave expert panel members reports on the innovations potentially ready for evaluation. Without knowing the names or locations of the programs and policies, the panel members rated each on (1) the innovation's promise and (2) the practicality of evaluation and its potential to employ rigorous design. Innovation promise included the expert panel's ratings about an innovation's reach or coverage of its target population, potential for changing the environment for children's eating or physical activity, potential for adoption, transportability and generalizability, feasibility of implementation, innovativeness, and acceptability to stakeholders. In rating an evaluation's practicality, experts assessed (1) the capacity of the developers and managers of the innovations to conduct or host an outcomes-focused evaluation, (2) the likelihood that the innovation would continue long enough for an outcomes-focused evaluation, and (3) data sources and possible evaluation designs. The project team aggregated results of the ratings and created graphs as an aid to facilitate the review discussion.

Expert Panel Meetings. In year one, the second review by the expert panel occurred in person, and, in year two, the panel members convened by telephone. The meeting began with three sets of questions:

- What are the foremost questions in the field concerning this topic?
- What are evaluation design options for programs or policies of this type (e.g., quasi-experiment, kinds of data available or accessible)?
- Considering the programs and policies reviewed, are there any particular programs to highlight in this area because of their unique or potentially powerful approach? What about innovations that exemplify a larger type or class of policies or programs?

Using these general overview questions, the meeting facilitator led the expert panel members through discussion of each innovation to determine which held promise for an evaluation and to make broad recommendations for particular evaluation approaches.

Rated Promise and Readiness for Outcomes-Focused Evaluation. In the first year, panel members discussed 16 innovations as potentially ready for outcomes-focused evaluation. The panel members eliminated innovations that did not seem to have high potential for positive health impact or had challenges that limited their readiness for outcomes-focused evaluation. This left a total of 9 innovations. In the second year the panel members discussed the 17 innovations presented to them and again eliminated innovations that did not seem to have high potential for positive health impact or were not ready for outcomes-focused evaluation. This left a total of 11 innovations. Across both years, the expert panel considered 20 innovations (4.4% of those initially nominated) to have high potential for positive health impact and to be ready for outcomes-focused evaluation. (See Table 2.3.)

After review of all innovations, the panel members voted for their top choices of innovations warranting further investment of resources for more rigorous, outcomes-focused evaluation. In the first year, the expert panel members began this discussion by identifying the thematic areas for innovation that they felt were priorities for evaluation. They selected day care, supermarket, and farmers' market innovations, but not school district local wellness policies or after-school settings. The panel members commented that day care is a focused target with a direct impact in preventing childhood obesity. They also considered supermarkets and farmers' markets significant areas for investigation, although their impact on childhood obesity is less proximal than day care, operating through the family's ability to purchase healthy foods. Children are more likely to eat lower-calorie foods when these foods are available in the home (Story et al., 2008). In year two the panel members did not discuss priority thematic areas and instead selected priority innovations directly after review of all the innovations.

In year one, each panel member was asked to select his or her two highest priorities and in year two to select the top three priority innovations. In both years of the project, most expert panel members felt three innovations had a much higher priority than the others for further evaluation, for a total of six priorities across the 2 years. In year one, the highest priority innovations were the Fresh Food Financing Initiative of the Food Trust of Philadelphia, and regulations on day care in New York City (enforced through inspections) to ensure healthy eating and physical activity. The third-rated priority in year one concerned an incentive program for low-income residents to purchase food at farmers' markets. In year two, the top-ranked priorities were a nationwide effort to construct playgrounds in vulnerable communities, a citywide policy to include calorie labeling on restaurant menus, and a statewide policy for after-school programs. (In year two, there was also some interest in a supermarket product rating program and a day care staff training program.) Following the votes, the expert panel discussed evaluation design possibilities for each of the highest priority innovations.

Step 6: Use of Information. The final step in the SSA Method is making use of the information in three ways: offering feedback to the developers of the innovations, sharing what has been learned about the topic areas assessed, and positioning the most promising innovations for outcomes-focused evaluation.

Tailored, Constructive Feedback and Technical Assistance to Developers of the Innovations. In addition to the evaluability assessment reports, the Early Assessment initiative gave stakeholders additional feedback and technical assistance. First, each visit closed with a "debriefing" discussion of preliminary findings about the policy or program being assessed, together with the primary contacts and any other stakeholders those contacts chose to invite. During the discussions, the site visitors reviewed their revised logic models and gained clarity on stakeholders' perceptions of activities and desired outcomes. The groups also discussed ideas for evaluation questions the stakeholders would most want to answer if resources became available for a formal evaluation.

Expanding on conventional EA, the initiative project team supplemented EA feedback by offering technical assistance follow-up phone calls to the innovation stakeholders. Representatives from the CDC served as content experts who reviewed the reports, participated in the phone calls, and made any recommendations that appeared to be useful to strengthen the innovations. The evaluability assessment teams also recommended some ways in which each innovation could better prepare for evaluation.

Synthesis Reports on Clusters of Innovations. To advance the field of obesity prevention research, the Early Assessment project team developed synthesis reports describing challenges and opportunities for programs and policies. The project team shared these reports with the primary contacts for each innovation assessed (Cheung, Dawkins, Kettel Khan, & Leviton, 2009; Pitt Barnes, Robin, Dawkins, Leviton, & Kettel Khan, 2009a, 2009b; Skelton, Dawkins, Leviton, & Kettel Khan, 2009; Wethington, Hall, Dawkins, Leviton, & Kettel Khan, 2009). The reports (soon to be posted at http://www.cdc.gov/nccdphp/dnpao) describe the typical achievements, opportunities, technical assistance needs, and ways to strengthen the innovations.

Feedback Survey of Visited Innovators. After the conclusion of all the year one and year two EAs and distribution of the synthesis reports, the project team conducted a brief survey with primary contacts at each of the visited innovations. For the most part, these contacts found the process helpful and reported that the logic model, summary report, and debriefing discussion of preliminary findings and evaluation ideas were most useful. They considered the synthesis report and the technical assistance follow-up phone calls somewhat useful as well (see Chapter 5 for details).

Positioning the Most Promising Innovations for Rigorous Evaluation. The primary product of the second expert panel review was identification of the 20 innovations that merited further evaluation. Of these, one of the top priorities of year one, the New York City day care regulations, is currently undergoing evaluation of both implementation and behavioral outcomes. As of 2009, the CDC funded evaluation of two other priorities, and two additional priorities are planned for evaluation in 2010. In addition, the project team developed a document for organizations that might be interested in funding those innovations for evaluation or further program development. It briefly described the initiative and all of the programs and policies that were considered promising. Also, the Prevention Research Center of the University of North Carolina, Chapel Hill, is in the process of posting the most promising innovations at their Center for Excellence in Training and Research Translation, in the category of "emerging interventions . . . that have been successfully implemented and show promise . . . but have not yet been fully evaluated in the field" (University of North Carolina Prevention Research Center, 2009). These actions should work to publicize the promise of the innovations while emphasizing that a formal evaluation is still required.

Value Added to the Field of Childhood Obesity Through SSA

The primary purpose of the Early Assessment initiative was to use the SSA Method to identify a high volume of promising innovations that were ready for evaluation. Such an effort was sorely needed in childhood obesity prevention, an area in which (as of 2009) there were only a limited number of tested interventions. The aim of the initiative was to jump-start this field of inquiry. The initiative has, arguably, achieved this goal. Of 458 original nominations, the expert panel considered 20 (4.4%) both to have high potential for positive health impact and to be ready for outcomes-focused evaluation. These innovations present the field with potential for practice-based evidence. If outcomes-focused evaluation shows them to be effective, they can then offer sound models for dissemination and replication.

Beyond its central purpose of identifying promising innovations, however, the initiative offered two other distinct kinds of value to the field of childhood obesity prevention. Because evaluability assessment is at the core of the SSA Method, the initiative was deliberately structured to supply the stakeholders for all 48 innovations with constructive information. The logic models, technical assistance provided on site, summary reports with recommendations, and follow-up technical assistance calls all aimed to assist the stakeholders with program or policy design, implementation, and readying the innovations for more rigorous outcomes focused evaluation.

Another type of value added was synthesis of what was learned across similar content-focused innovations. There is value in sharing information, not only about what seemed to be working in programs and policies but also about challenges in program or policy design and implementation to be avoided.

The SSA Method in Practice

Just as the Early Assessment initiative provided information regarding innovations in the field of childhood obesity prevention, it offered many lessons about the practical application of the SSA Method.

Moving From Concept to Reality. The overall plan for the SSA Method turned out to be sound. However, moving to actual implementation in the Early Assessment initiative showed where additional structure, not to mention a management plan, was essential to make the process work. For example, 458 nominations were simply not a digestible number for nationally recognized experts to review—especially when it emerged that so many did not meet inclusion criteria. To use the expert panel optimally, it was also important to summarize all the initial documents the project team had collected on the innovations. In the same way, if innovations were clearly not ready for evaluation, there was no point in presenting them as part of the

NEW DIRECTIONS FOR EVALUATION • DOI: 10.1002/ev

second expert review panel process. Uniformity of training, report templates, and procedures all were necessary to make the SSA Method concept work in practice.

Challenges and Adaptations of the SSA Method. Almost every step in the SSA Method presented challenges. In the first step of the method, the project team worked hard to interest national stakeholders in the concept. Because it had never been tried before, this process required considerable orchestration. Before the launch of the initiative, representatives of CDC and NIH, together with experts in evaluation and childhood obesity prevention research, participated in a review of the proposed method. This process gave them an understanding of the reasons for the SSA Method and some buy-in for selection of key themes and topics. This step also legitimized SSA for the expert panel that was assembled for the Early Assessment initiative. It was critically important to identify and engage an expert panel with varying perspectives and expertise (for example, in nutrition, physical activity, environmental and policy approaches, and evaluation). The diverse panel helped to ensure that a range of relevant issues were considered.

The second step in the method is to request nominations and use the established criteria to determine those eligible for the panel members' review. A significant challenge lay in identifying enough relevant programs and policies. We found that engaging an array of interest groups and scanning the literature and the Internet yielded a substantial list of nominations. However, the challenges at this step were analogous to those of a screening test for disease: there were problems of both sensitivity and specificity.

Initially, the nominations process was not *sensitive* enough to locate innovations outside of mainstream health education and promotion. This problem was mitigated in year two on the basis of experience. In both years, the Early Assessment initiative project team reached out to contact some potential innovations to encourage their participation—particularly when that innovation's sphere of practice appeared less directly associated with the health-related outcome of interest. For example, the developers of supermarket innovations may not see their relationship to childhood obesity but rather focus on economic goals. They are also unlikely to have professional networks that include health educators.

The year one nominations process also was overly sensitive and not *specific* enough for the mainstream health promotion topic of local wellness policies. The initiative received a flood of nominations, but many of them were not suitable, for various reasons. By offering more specific guidance on nominations, we mitigated this problem somewhat in year two for CSPA innovations. Yet overall, the ultimate yield from these two topics was quite small.

Another challenge at this step lay in getting the innovators to participate. Some were interested in the altruistic goal of advancing the field of childhood obesity prevention by sharing their successes and learning about the successes of others. For others the offer of technical assistance helped generate their willingness to participate. Most innovators were interested in

NEW DIRECTIONS FOR EVALUATION • DOI: 10.1002/ev

the potential for future funding if their innovation was determined "promising" or if they were selected to be evaluated. After the year one visits, a number of innovators were able to use sections of the EA summary reports in grant applications for additional funding. In year two, sharing this experience helped encourage innovators to participate.

In the third step of the SSA Method, expert panel members must review innovations to make selections for evaluability assessments. Summaries of innovations were fairly brief at this stage because of the need to balance the large number of nominations with the burden on the panel members. Thus the expert panel needed to make these decisions on the basis of limited information. Initially they were hesitant about making selections using limited data. However, they were encouraged by the knowledge that the screening process ruled interesting ideas in, while clearly flawed ideas were ruled out.

Step 4 in the method involves engaging a broad network of professionals to conduct the evaluability assessments. A significant challenge of this step was to ensure uniformity across all stages of those assessments on the part of various site visitors. Centralized oversight to retain the method's integrity proved important to manage multiple concurrent evaluability assessment visits and to ensure consistency in the protocol and reporting used by site visitors across multiple sites (see Chapter 3 for details).

Implications for Future Use of the SSA Method and Evaluability Assessments

From experience with the Early Assessment initiative, we can make some observations on the applicability of the SSA Method. It has demonstrated its potential to speed up evaluation of advances in childhood obesity prevention, where limited science exists regarding innovations that can help slow or reverse the obesity trend. The method is likely to do so under similar conditions in other fields, or whenever little is known about innovative practices. Unknown at this time is whether SSA holds promise in areas where science may be strong but translation to practice has been weak. However, the method is likely to be helpful in such areas because of the clear need for more knowledge of necessary adaptations, given diverse settings, populations, and resources. On the basis of this initial application, the SSA Method appears to hold promise for increasing the yield from evaluations.

References

Cheung, K., Dawkins, N., Kettel Khan, L., & Leviton, L. C. (2009). *Early Assessment of Programs and Policies to Prevent Childhood Obesity: Synthesis of initiatives that increase access to healthy foods.* Atlanta: U.S. Department of Health and Human Services, Centers for Disease Control and Prevention.

Child Nutrition and WIC Reauthorization Act of 2004, Section 204 of Public Law 108–265.

Guide to Community Preventive Services. (2009). *Promoting physical activity: Environmental and policy approaches*. Retrieved from http://www.thecommunityguide.org/pa/environmental-policy/index.html. Last updated February 10, 2009.

Heath, G. W., Brownson, R. C., Kruger, J., Miles, R., Powell, K. E., Ramsey, L. T., et al. (2006). The effectiveness of urban design and land use and transport policies and practices to increase physical activity: A systematic review. *Journal of Physical Activity and Health, 3*(Suppl. 1), S55–76.

Koplan, J. P., Liverman, C. T., & Kraak, V. I. (Eds.). (2001). *Preventing childhood obesity: Health in the* balance. Washington, DC: National Academies Press.

Leviton, L. C., Kettel-Khan, L., Rog, D., Dawkins, N., & Cotton, D. (in press). Evaluability assessment to improve public health. *Annual Review of Public Health.*

National Association for Sport and Physical Education. (2008). *Comprehensive school physical activity programs*. (Position statement.) Reston, VA: Author.

Ogden, C. L., Carroll, M. D., Curtin, L. R., McDowell, M. A., Tabak, C. J., & Flegal, K. M. (2006). Prevalence of overweight and obesity in the United States, 1999–2004. *JAMA, 295,* 1549–1555.

Pitt Barnes, S., Robin, L., Dawkins, N., Leviton, L., & Kettel Khan, L. (2009a). *Early Assessment of Programs and Policies to Prevent Childhood Obesity Evaluability Assessment Synthesis Report: Comprehensive school physical activity programs*. Atlanta: U.S. Department of Health and Human Services, Centers for Disease Control and Prevention.

Pitt Barnes, S., Robin, L., Dawkins, N., Leviton, L. C., & Kettel Khan, L. (2009b). *Early Assessment of Programs and Policies to Prevent Childhood Obesity Evaluability Assessment Synthesis Report: Local wellness policy*. Atlanta: U.S. Department of Health and Human Services, Centers for Disease Control and Prevention.

Skelton, S., Dawkins, N., Leviton, L., & Kettel Khan, L. (2009). *Early Assessment of Programs and Policies to Prevent Childhood Obesity Evaluability Assessment Synthesis Brief: Built environment and land use programs*. Atlanta: U.S. Department of Health and Human Services, Centers for Disease Control and Prevention.

Story, M., Kaphingst, K. M., & French, S. (2006). The role of childcare settings in obesity prevention. *The Future of Children, 16,* 143–168.

Story, M., Kaphingst, K. M., Robinson-O'Brien, R., & Glanz, K. (2008). Creating healthy food and eating environments: Policy and environmental approaches. *Annual Review of Public Health, 29,* 253–272.

University of North Carolina Prevention Research Center. (2009). *Obesity prevention program: Emerging interventions*. Retrieved May 29, 2009, from http://www.center-trt.org/index.cfm?fa=op.overview

Wang, Y. C., Gortmaker, S. L., Sobol, A. M., & Kuntz, K. M. (2006). Estimating the energy gap among U.S. children: A counterfactual approach. *Pediatrics, 118*(6). Retrieved from http://www.pediatrics.org/cgi/content/full/118/6/e1721

Wechsler, H., McKenna, M. L., Lee, S. M., & Deitz, W. H. (2004). The role of schools in preventing childhood obesity. Retrieved February 7, 2010, from http://www.cdc.gov/HealthyYouth/physicalactivity/pdf/roleofschools_obesity.pdf

Wethington, H., Hall, M. A., Dawkins, N., Leviton, L., & Kettel Khan, L. (2009). *Early Assessment of Programs and Policies to Prevent Childhood Obesity Evaluability Assessment Synthesis Report: Childcare initiatives in afterschool and daycare settings*. Atlanta: U.S. Department of Health and Human Services, Centers for Disease Control and Prevention.

Wholey, J. S. (1979). *Evaluation: Promise and performance*. Washington, DC: Urban Institute.

Wholey, J. S. (2004). Evaluability assessment. In J. S. Wholey, H. P. Hatry, & K. E. Newcomer, *Handbook of practical program evaluation* (pp. 33–62). San Francisco: Jossey-Bass.

NICOLA DAWKINS is a Principal at ICF Macro, where she designs and implements research and evaluation studies and led ICF Macro's team in coordinating the Robert Wood Johnson Foundation/CDC initiative Early Assessment of Programs and Policies to Prevent Childhood Obesity.

HOLLY WETHINGTON is a Behavioral Scientist on the Research and Surveillance Team in the Division of Nutrition, Physical Activity, and Obesity at the Centers for Disease Control and Prevention (CDC).

LAURA KETTEL KHAN is currently the Senior Scientist for Policy and Partnerships in the Division of Nutrition, Physical Activity, and Obesity at the Centers for Disease Control and Prevention (CDC), the primary public health agency working to prevent obesity and chronic diseases in the United States.

JO ANNE GRUNBAUM is a Health Scientist and Team Lead of the Research and Evaluation Team in the Prevention Research Centers, Division of Adult and Community Health at the Centers for Disease Control and Prevention.

LEAH ROBIN is a Health Scientist, Division of Adolescent and School Health, at the Centers for Disease Control and Prevention (CDC).

SERAPHINE PITT BARNES is a Health Scientist in the Division of Adolescent and School Health at the Centers for Disease Control and Prevention (CDC).

DAVID COTTON is a Senior Vice President of ICF Macro's Applied Research Division, where his work focuses on research, evaluation, and evaluation capacity building in public health.

DIANE O. DUNET is the Team Lead, Evaluation and Program Effectiveness Team, Division for Heart Disease and Stroke Prevention at the Centers for Disease Control and Prevention (CDC) and developer of the Swift Worksite Assessment and Translation (SWAT) method referenced in this issue.

LAURA C. LEVITON is the coauthor of Foundations of Program Evaluation *and is currently Special Advisor for Evaluation at the Robert Wood Johnson Foundation, where for the past 10 years she has overseen more than 80 evaluations at the national, state, and local levels.*

NEW DIRECTIONS FOR EVALUATION • DOI: 10.1002/ev

Osuji, T. A., Dawkins, N., & Rice, S. M. (2010). Training and support for evaluability assessment methodology. In L. C. Leviton, L. Kettel Khan, & N. Dawkins (Eds.), *The Systematic Screening and Assessment Method: Finding innovations worth evaluating. New Directions for Evaluation, 125,* 51–66.

3

Training and Support for Evaluability Assessment Methodology

Thearis A. Osuji, Nicola Dawkins, Starr M. Rice

Abstract

The authors describe training of a network of professionals to conduct evaluability assessments for the Early Assessment of Programs and Policies on Childhood Obesity Initiative (Early Assessment Initiative). We learned that (1) the professionals trained had a diverse set of skills and expertise, (2) a training refresher session solidified methods and concepts, (3) evaluability assessments were improved when training included content on qualitative interviewing and development and application of logic models, and (4) comprehensive and consistent training methods helped to ensure consistency and methodological integrity © Wiley Periodicals, Inc., and the American Evaluation Association.

In 2007, the Early Assessment Initiative sought to develop a network of evaluation and public health professionals with the skills to conduct evaluability assessments (EAs). EA gauges whether a program is plausible and feasible by identifying issues related to designing and implementing program components, assessing data systems and the capacity to collect relevant data, and determining whether key elements of the program are

consistent with the program's theory. EA involves clarifying goals, elaborating program design by specifying the program or policy model, finding out stakeholders' views on the important issues, and exploring program or policy reality (Wholey, 2004). The most common methods used in EA are document review, interviews, and site visits to observe the program or policy (Trevisan, 2007). The initiative researchers created a protocol for EA that incorporated all of these methods.

To participate in the initiative, the project team actively sought evaluation and public health professionals with skills and experience in methods applicable to EA. Professionals with expertise related to obesity prevention programs were preferred, but this was not a requirement. Trainees came from the project team's organizations: the Robert Wood Johnson Foundation, Centers for Disease Control and Prevention (CDC), CDC Foundation, and ICF Macro. In addition, nine researchers from CDC's university-affiliated Prevention Research Centers were invited to participate. In all, 32 individuals participated in the full in-person training in year one; an additional 8 individuals participated in a minitraining webinar session in year two.

As seen in Table 3.1, the trainees from year one had a range of skills and areas of expertise. All of the trainees had a minimum of a master's degree, and many had a doctorate in a field such as public health, sociology,

Table 3.1. Expertise and Skills of the Professionals Trained in Evaluability Assessment Methodology

Area of Expertise	n (%)
Evaluation	23 (72)
Nutrition	13 (41)
Physical activity	13 (41)
School-aged youth	14 (44)
Day care	7 (22)
Farmers' markets	5 (16)
Other programs related to increasing access to healthier foods and beverages	5 (16)

Skills	n (%)
Logic modeling:	
High	5 (16)
Medium-high	5 (16)
Medium	17 (53)
Low-medium	2 (6)
Low	0
Fluency in a foreign language:	
Spanish	4
Cantonese	1
German	1

Note: N = 32. Items are not mutually exclusive; therefore, the total number and percentage of responses are not cumulative.

psychology, or education. The training process and the EAs afforded substantial opportunities for the evaluators to learn from one another. The project team assigned two site visitors to each program or policy EA, and to capitalize on diversity the pair had complementary expertise.

Training and Support Methods

Training and support for the EA site visitors was an ongoing, iterative effort. This process involved a 2-day, in-person training workshop, a comprehensive EA protocol with numerous guides and templates, technical support from content-area experts and core project team members, and a webinar refresher session.

In-Person Training Workshop. The first step was a 2-day workshop where the primary objective was to train participants in the EA protocol designed for the Early Assessment Initiative. Consistent with adult learning theory (Knowles, 1980), the workshop fostered an interactive learning environment that allowed the participants to build on their existing skills and experiences, share that experience, and learn from one another. The major components of the workshop included:

- *Background and purpose of the Early Assessment Initiative.* To begin, the workshop facilitators described the issue of childhood obesity, reviewed the history of the initiative, and gave an overview of the project.
- *Overview of evaluability assessments.* Workshop facilitators presented an overview of the historical roots of evaluability assessments, discussed their goals, differentiated EAs from full-scale evaluations, summarized the EA process, and described how EA fits within CDC's Framework for Program Evaluation (CDC, 1999).
- *In-depth review of the EA protocol.* Participants discussed the EA protocol in great detail for about a day. Using a combination of lecture and large-group discussion, various presenters walked workshop participants through each step of the EA protocol. As appropriate, the workshop facilitators and participants shared their experiences in conducting evaluability assessments or any of the components of the evaluability assessment process (document review, logic models, site visits, providing technical assistance, etc.).
- *Qualitative interviews review.* This session involved an overview of tips for conducting individual interviews and an in-depth review of each of the qualitative interview guides. Participants also shared their experiences and tips for conducting qualitative interviews.
- *Logic modeling primer.* Two evaluators with expertise in developing and employing logic models led this exercise in using logic models to conduct evaluability assessments. The facilitators described logic models and their application in program evaluation and then guided trainees through the process of developing a logic model. Throughout the primer, the facilitators

highlighted the specific application of logic modeling to evaluability assessments and the Early Assessment Initiative.

Materials and Templates. Consistency in application of the methods used was critical for this project, because the primary objective of the Early Assessment Initiative was to conduct EAs of numerous promising programs and policies addressing childhood obesity. To do this, the core project team developed a detailed, comprehensive EA protocol with numerous appendices containing guides and templates for use by the EA teams. The protocol included these components:

- *Project overview* of the Early Assessment Initiative and the SSA Method, outlining project objectives and questions to guide the EAs.
- *Pre-site visit procedures,* containing detailed, step-by-step instructions for tasks preceding the site visit component, a timeline of activities (see Table 3.2), procedures and recommendations for reviewing program documents, and instructions for developing a draft program or policy logic model. Also included was a logistics guide, with instructions for working with the site visit coordinator and the local site liaison for the EA, identifying appropriate program or policy informants, scheduling interviews and procedures, and making travel arrangements.
- *Site visit field procedures,* outlining the roles and responsibilities of the EA team onsite. Also included were guidelines for interviewing program and policy representatives, procedures for maintaining data security, and recommendations for troubleshooting unanticipated issues onsite.
- *Post-site visit procedures,* containing a timeline of activities (as illustrated in Table 3.3), procedures for communication with the site (thank-you letters and guidance for a follow-up technical assistance call), and report preparation (guidance on data management, preparation, and analysis).
- *Qualitative interview guides* for each program and policy assessed. The guide included an introduction and informed consent statement and questions concerning a program or policy's history, stakeholders, design, implementation, resources, funding, and evaluation or data collection activities.
- *Environmental assessment guide,* designed to help EA teams assess aspects of the physical environment and activities when observing a program or policy in action. The guide contained seven sections: assessment of a building, indoor facilities, outdoor facilities, food environment, program participants, neighborhood assessment, and other comments.
- *Report outlines and templates* (see Table 3.4 for sample outline), which standardized the EA reports. Because the Early Assessment Initiative involved assessing the promise and readiness for evaluation of multiple programs and policies, standardized reporting procedures were critical. These materials helped EA teams develop a topline summary and a full summary report.

NEW DIRECTIONS FOR EVALUATION • DOI: 10.1002/ev

Minimum Time Frame	ICF Macro Coordinator	EA Site Visitor
X weeks prior to site visit	Introductory letter Invitation to participate Request preferred dates Follow-up phone call one Overview of site visit process Request program/policy documents Determine dates of the site visit Assign site visitors	
X weeks prior to site visit	Confirmation e-mail one Confirm dates for site visit Send instructions for determining interviewees	Begin draft logic model Review program/policy documents
X weeks prior to site visit	Follow-up phone call two Follow up on outstanding program/policy documents Discuss the suggested site informants and finalize list of persons to interview Confirm site visit logistics (approximate start and ending times needed to make travel arrangements) E-mail scheduling template to program/policy liaison Travel arrangements Confirm dates, nearest airport, determine if rental car is needed as appropriate Prepare and submit travel request form Confirmation letter two Confirm final site visit schedule	Follow-up phone call two (with ICF Macro Coordinating Center and program/policy contact) Follow up on outstanding program/policy documents Discuss the suggested site informants and finalize list of persons to interview Confirm site visit logistics (approximate start and ending times needed to make travel arrangements) Travel arrangements Follow up with agency to make travel arrangements Furnish credit card information to reserve lodging Give ICF Macro coordinator copy of itinerary AIRLINE TICKETS MUST BE BOOKED AT LEAST 14 DAYS PRIOR TO DEPARTURE
X weeks prior to site visit	Send additional materials to site visitors Any remaining background documents or materials Copies of travel itineraries for both site visitors	
X weeks prior to site visit	Review draft logic model	Draft logic model due Confirm final logistics with site as necessary Addresses and directions Other questions

Table 3.3. Timeline of Post-Site Visit Activities

Minimum Time Frame	EA Site Visitors	ICF Macro Coordinator
X weeks after site visit	Input to thank-you letter Confirm final list of persons interviewed Contact ICF Macro Coordinating Center if wish to tailor standard thank-you letter	Finalize thank-you letters and have the letters sent to interviewees
X weeks after site visit	Topline summary report due Begin work on draft summary report and recommendations Complete any outstanding telephone interviews so data can be included in analysis and site visit reports	Review topline summary report and request revisions from site visitors as needed Post topline summary report on shared website
X weeks after site visit	Draft summary report due Provide ICF Macro Coordinating Center with detailed draft site visit summary report Draft recommendations due	Share draft summary report with lead program/policy administrator After internal review, send draft site visit report to lead program/policy administrator to check for any factual errors Share draft recommendations with CDC content area expert(s) for review
X weeks after site visit	Revise draft summary report on receipt of feedback Revise draft recommendations on receipt of feedback	Return reviewed summary report to site visitors on receipt from lead program/policy administrator Return reviewed recommendations to site visitors on receipt of feedback from CDC content expert(s)
X weeks after site visit	Revised summary report due to ICF Macro Coordinating Center Revised recommendations due to ICF Macro Coordinating Center	Finalize summary report After internal review send revised summary report to ICF Macro Publications for editing, formatting, and finishing services Add recommendations as a section to the final summary report Schedule technical assistance consultation call
X weeks after site visit	Follow-up technical assistance consultation call	Share finalized summary report with program/policy lead administrator Final summary report includes the recommendations as a section Follow-up technical assistance consultation Conduct 1-hour telephone call with program/policy stakeholders to discuss recommendations for

Table 3.4. Summary Report Outline

Section	Contents and Questions to Answer	Relevant Information Sources
Cover page: (1 page)	Program/policy name Program type (after-school or day care program, local wellness policy, comprehensive school physical activity program, land use program, food access program—restaurant or supermarket/convenience store) Names of site visitors and dates of visit	N/A
Section I: *Background and Purpose of Evaluability Assessment* (1–2 pages)	Early Assessment of Programs and Policies to Prevent Childhood Obesity project background Definition of evaluability assessment Purpose of evaluability assessment	ICF Macro Coordinating Center provides standard language
Section II: *Methods* (1–2 pages)	Document review: • List of documents used Site visits: • Dates • Location • Persons interviewed (name and title) • Number of interviews • Average length of interviews Environmental assessment: • Describe notes from assessment	Site visit notebook Interview notes Environmental assessment notes

Section III: *Identified Elements of the Program/Policy (as Planned and as Implemented)* (5–7 pages)	Program/policy as planned:
	• Brief history or scope of the program/policy
	  • Duration
	  • Developed by whom? Why?
	• What are the planned components of the program or policy?
		Background documents
		Environmental assessment
		Responses to ALL interview questions in Sections I (*History*), II (*Describe the Program/Policy*), III (*Stakeholders*), and V (*Funding*)

(Continued)

Table 3.4. (Continued)

Section	Contents and Questions to Answer	Relevant Information Sources

	• What are the goals and expected outcomes of the program or policy?
	• Who is the planned target audience?
	
	Program/policy as implemented:
	• Have there been any major shifts in the program design since inception or planning?
	• Was the program/policy pilot-tested? Full implementation for how long?
	• Scope: Geographic breadth, number of participants, schools, children, consumers, etc.
	  • Frequency, duration, and amount of component activities
	  • Staffing of components and overall
	  • Actual, active partners
	  • Products, outputs
	• How far has implementation of the program progressed?
	• Is the program/policy accessing the same target audience as planned? Is the program/policy tailored to the target audience? If so, how was it tailored to them?
	• How is the program/policy funded? Other salient resources (staffing, etc)?
	
	Program/Policy Context:
	• Organizational context for the program/policy (size, type, placement of program/policy within larger organization, duration of organization's existence, rate of main staff turnover, etc.)
	• Community context of the program/policy. Briefly describe the surrounding community (e.g., demographics, SES). Is the community involved with the program/policy? How?	

Section IV: *Highlighted Findings* (1–3 pages)	Plausibility: • To what extent is the program/policy based on scientific theory or evidence? • Is there agreement on the program/policy logic model among key stakeholders? Feasibility: • What evidence is there of the feasibility of the program/policy being implemented fully as intended? • What are the resources (time, staffing, financial, etc.) available and required to implement the program/policy?	Responses to ALL interview questions in Section I (*History*), Section II (*Describe the Program/Policy*), and V (*Funding*) Program/policy logic model
Section V: *Evaluation Potential* (1–3 pages)	Report of observations for evaluation capacity building: • Is there an ongoing documentation or formal evaluation component? • What are available data sources? • What is the perceived need for evaluation by key staff?	Data documentation Responses to ALL interview questions in Section IV (*Evaluation*)
Section VI: *Recommendations* (1–2 pages)	Briefly note program current strengths in each area and provide suggestions for future program planning: • Goals • Audience • Funding/resources • Program design • Infrastructure • Organizational support • Community support • Underlying theory and scientific evidence • Data collection, monitoring, and evaluation	Responses to ALL interview questions from ALL sections Observations from environmental assessment
Section VII: *Conclusion* (1–2 pages)	• Brief summary of results • Highlight key findings	N/A
Appendices	• Program/policy logic model • guide topics	

- *Example program and policy logic models,* which helped the teams develop logic models in the context of EA. Examples were presented for each of the program types assessed: increasing access to healthier foods and beverages, school district local wellness policies, after-school and day care programs, built environment projects, and comprehensive school physical activity programs. Each example logic model contained content suggestions for consideration: a problem statement, inputs, activities, outputs, short-term outcomes, intermediate outcomes, long-term outcomes, goals, and contextual factors. Figures 3.1, 3.2, and 3.3 present the examples for after-school and day care, supermarket and convenience store interventions, and school district local wellness policies.

Technical Support. Most participants had research and evaluation expertise, but technical expertise in disciplines related to childhood obesity prevention varied. The core project team therefore identified CDC scientists with subject matter expertise in the program and policy types that were the focus of this project. The subject matter experts offered two critical services to assist the teams as they conducted EAs: (1) advice, consultation, and resources to the teams conducting the EAs; and (2) technical assistance to the developers of the programs and policies undergoing EA. Project coordinators facilitated a conference call with the EA teams and the subject matter experts prior to the Early Assessment Initiative site visits. In the conference call, the subject matter experts shared the key components of programs and policies within the topic area, tips for items or issues to look for during site visits, and suggestions for gathering information from program and policy staff members.

The project leadership assigned a coordinator for each program or policy type to oversee the EAs and provide technical support to EA teams. These coordinators helped to facilitate the process through frequent communication with the EA teams and with the local liaisons for the programs or policies undergoing EA. The coordinators guided the site visitors through the process, helped obtain documents for review and reminded EA teams of deadlines and key milestones. The coordinators also served as a link between the site visitors and the core team for the initiative, as well as other site visitors. If the coordinator could not answer a site visitor's questions or concerns about any aspect of the evaluability assessment, he or she consulted the core team and communicated the response back to the site visitor.

Webinar Refresher Session. After the first year of the initiative, the training facilitators conducted a webinar refresher session for all EA teams. This helped to prepare the EA teams for a second round of EAs. The refresher session included a review of site visitor responsibilities, an in-depth review of changes to the EA protocol, a discussion of options for furnishing technical assistance to program or policy staff as part of the EA process, and a refresher on qualitative interviewing. The webinar facilitators allowed ample time for the EA teams to share with one another their experiences from the first round of EAs and give each other tips and suggestions

NEW DIRECTIONS FOR EVALUATION • DOI: 10.1002/ev

Figure 3.1. After-School and Day Care Programs (and Related Policies)

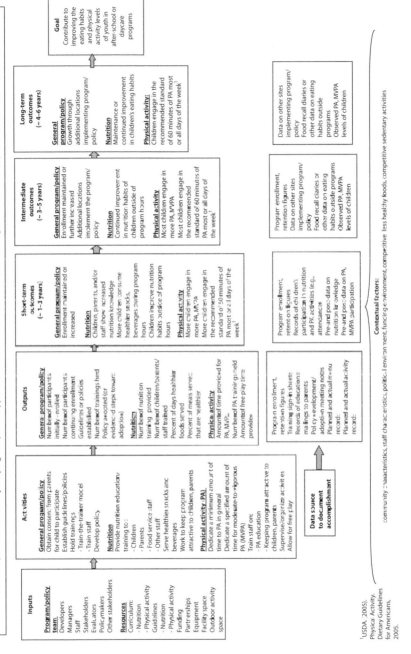

Figure 3.2. Access to Healthier Foods: Supermarkets and Convenience Stores

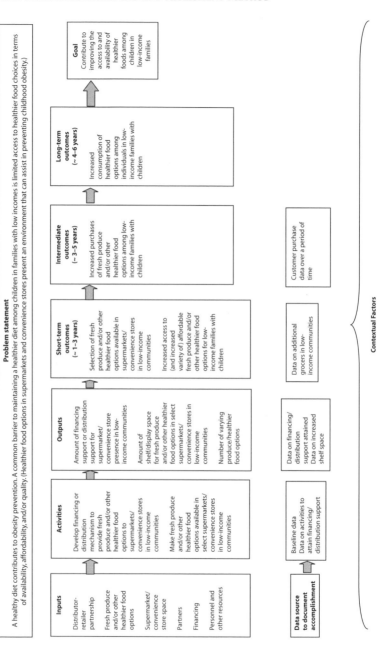

Figure 3.3. School District Local Wellness Policy

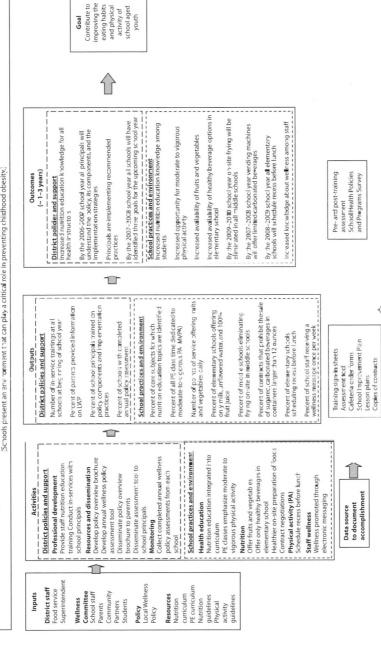

for conducting EAs. This training session was also an opportunity to address the issues that arose in the results from a survey concerning the EA training process.

Survey of EA Teams

The core project team administered a survey to assess the effectiveness of training efforts and to inform future EA training activities. EA teams responded to the survey via email about the training, materials, and technical support. Approximately 50% of the EA teams responded to the survey. As shown in Table 3.5, site visitor feedback concerning the training, materials, and technical support was positive overall.

Three items in particular stood out to the core project team as aspects of the training workshop and materials that needed additional attention: (1) review of interviewing tips, (2) development of logic models, and (3) the environmental assessment guide. A few comments suggested that a role-play session would have been beneficial in the review of interviewing tips. A session was originally planned for day two of the workshop, but it was cut

Table 3.5. Results of the Early Assessment Training Process Survey

Item	Mean
Feedback on components of the training workshop:	
Review of evaluability assessments and differentiation from full-scale evaluation	4.5
Presentation on project background	4.2
Review of data management and data security	4.2
Review of EA steps for the project	4.1
Review of data analysis and report writing	4.1
Review of site visit interview questions	4.1
Review of lead and support site visitor roles and responsibilities	3.9
Providing technical assistance to the program or policy developers and managers	3.9
Review of interview tips	3.7
Review on developing logic models	3.7
Feedback on materials and resources received:	
Training materials and site visit protocol	4.2
Interview guides	4.0
Environmental assessment guide	3.6
Feedback on technical support received:	
Communication with area coordinator after the site visit regarding reporting procedures	4.7
Communication with program or policy thematic area coordinator prior to the site visit	4.5
Communication with area coordinator during the site visit	4.5
Program or policy content area conference call with technical expert	4.2

Note: $N = 16$. This table includes the results from participants in year one of the project. Mean: 1 = *needs significant improvement*; 2 = *needs some improvement*; 3 = *worked OK*; 4 = *worked well*; 5 = *worked very well.*

because of time constraints. Comments on the logic model discussion suggested that more clarity was needed on application of the logic models in the site visitors' discussion with program or policy stakeholders. Site visitor comments indicated that, overall, the environmental assessment guide was too long and perhaps too tedious for the brief observations appropriate for EAs.

Discussion: Key Insights From the Training Process

The Early Assessment Initiative team identified four key insights that resulted from the process of training public health and evaluation professionals in EA methodology.

Including public health and evaluation professionals with a diverse set of skills and expertise helps to enhance the training process. Throughout the training process the initiative staff recognized the tremendous benefit of bringing together evaluation and public health professionals with diverse skills and experiences. Although most of the professionals who were trained had limited or no experience with evaluability assessments, each EA team brought unique skills and experiences that added value to the process. Some professionals had a strong background in logic modeling; others contributed greatly from their skills and experiences with other key methods used in EA, such as qualitative interviewing, providing technical assistance to program or project staff, or knowledge of childhood obesity prevention. To take advantage of this diversity in skills and expertise, the training facilitators felt it was important to incorporate substantial time in every phase of the training process for discussion among participants.

A refresher session, either in person or using a Web-based format, allows training facilitators to reinforce the key concepts associated with EA and is an opportunity for EA teams to learn from one another's experiences in conducting EAs. A refresher session imparts two critical benefits to any training or educational effort. It creates an opportunity for educators to reinforce critical skills, and a forum that allows EA teams to learn from one another's experiences. In the Early Assessment Initiative, we found that one year into the project, after each of the EA teams had completed at least one EA, was an ideal time for a refresher session.

Qualitative interviewing and development and application of logic models are key research and evaluation methodologies that must be reinforced in EA training. For the Early Assessment Initiative, the training facilitators intended only to review qualitative interviews and logic models. Because we selected evaluation and public health professionals with graduate education and some experience in program evaluation, we assumed that the participants in our training sessions would have at least an introductory level of experience with these methods. This assumption did not hold true for all the EA teams; consequently, we needed to invest more time training on these components of EA. This observation, coupled with the findings from our training process survey, suggests a need for additional training in application of program logic models and qualitative interviewing in EA training, and perhaps additional emphasis in professional evaluation training programs.

Comprehensive and consistent training help to ensure consistency and methodological integrity in applying the Systematic Screening and Assessment Method. The Early Assessment project staff found that having a comprehensive training process, which included an in-person training workshop, refresher session, extensive materials and templates, and technical support for EA teams, made an invaluable contribution to the entire Early Assessment Initiative.

References

Centers for Disease Control and Prevention (CDC). (1999). Framework for program evaluation in public health. *MMWR. Recommendations and reports: Morbidity and Mortality Weekly Report, 48*(RR-11), 140.

Knowles, M. (1980). *The modern practice of adult education.* New York: Cambridge University Press.

Trevisan, M. S. (2007). Evaluability assessment from 1986 to 2006. *American Journal of Evaluation, 28*(3), 290–303.

Wholey, J. S. (2004). Evaluability assessment. In J. S. Wholey, H. P. Hatry, & K. E. Newcomer (Eds.), *Handbook of practical program evaluation* (2nd ed., pp. 33–62). San Francisco: Jossey-Bass.

THEARIS A. OSUJI is a Senior Associate at ICF Macro.

NICOLA DAWKINS is a Principal at ICF Macro, where she designs and implements research and evaluation studies and led ICF Macro's team in coordinating the Robert Wood Johnson Foundation/CDC initiative Early Assessment of Programs and Policies to Prevent Childhood Obesity.

STARR M. RICE is a Research Technician at ICF Macro.

Pitt Barnes, S., Wethington, H., & Cheung, K. (2010). Early Assessment Initiative using the Systematic Screening and Assessment Method: Three case studies. In L. C. Leviton, L. Kettel Khan, & N. Dawkins (Eds.), *The Systematic Screening and Assessment Method: Finding innovations worth evaluating. New Directions for Evaluation, 125,* 67–93.

4

Early Assessment Initiative Using the Systematic Screening and Assessment Method: Three Case Studies

Seraphine Pitt Barnes, Holly Wethington, Karen Cheung

Abstract

Three case studies describe how the Systematic Screening and Assessment (SSA) Method was used to identify innovations that hold promise to prevent childhood obesity. Nominations were reviewed by an expert panel; those having the greatest potential and therefore meriting closer examination through evaluability assessment were identified, and finally the panel chose those that were promising and ready for evaluation. The three case examples are the Fresh Food Financing Initiative of the Food Trust of Philadelphia; New York City's regulations to enforce healthy eating and physical activity in 1,600 licensed day care centers; and the Natrona County, Wyoming, School District local wellness policy. © Wiley Periodicals, Inc., and the American Evaluation Association.

Note: The findings and conclusions in this report are those of the authors and do not necessarily represent the official position of the Centers for Disease Control and Prevention.

One-third of youth in the United States are overweight or obese, presenting significant public health problems (Ogden, Carroll, & Flegal, 2008). In response, U.S. communities and schools are developing and implementing programs and policies to stem this epidemic. The programs aim to affect children's daily physical activity, their food intake, or both. The Early Assessment of Programs and Policies to Prevent Childhood Obesity was a 2-year initiative that used the Systematic Screening and Assessment (SSA) Method to identify promising local-level childhood obesity prevention innovations and then assess whether they were ready to be evaluated. The initiative aimed to assess innovations affecting children 3 to 17 years of age.

Assessing the evaluation readiness of childhood obesity prevention innovations is a critical first step to determine effectiveness and ensure the judicious use of scarce evaluation resources. Evaluability assessment (EA), a cornerstone of the SSA Method, involves clarifying goals and program design by specifying the program or policy logic, determining stakeholder views on the important issues, and exploring program or policy reality (Wholey, 2004).

However, the SSA Method uses EA to gauge promise by assessing the plausibility of the logic model, the theory of change underlying program activities, and the feasibility of implementing the innovation. Plausibility is the scientific basis by which we would expect an environmental innovation to cause individual-level behavioral changes and health outcomes (Leviton, Kettel Khan, Rog, Dawkins, & Cotton, in press). Feasibility is the likelihood that the environmental innovation, as designed, could be implemented fully and faithfully in the original setting and in other venues. Evaluators assess whether an innovation is feasible by identifying implementation issues about program or policy components and by determining whether key elements of the program or policy are consistent with the logic model or theory of change. Other criteria for assessing an innovation's promise are coverage of the target population, generalizability to other populations, acceptability to stakeholders, cost, and feasibility of implementation by others.

During the first year of the Early Assessment Initiative, the Funders Advisory Committee (program officers of CDC, NIH, USDA, and private foundations) identified thematic areas needing further study. These areas represented opportunities for environmental changes to influence children's eating and physical activity. The case studies presented in this chapter are examples from three areas identified by the committee:

1. Innovative food access programs seek to increase access to healthier foods in low-income, inner-city communities. These innovations include programs to provide healthy offerings in farmers' markets, restaurants, supermarkets, and corner stores.
2. Programs and policies for child care in after-school and day care settings can affect what children eat and the amount of time they are physically

active during the day. Child care serves a captive population and reaches a large proportion of lower-income children.

3. School district local wellness policies have been mandated by federal law since 2006 (Child Nutrition and Women, Infants, and Children [WIC] Reauthorization Act of 2004). Federal law requires school districts that participate in federally funded meal programs to establish nutritional guidelines for all foods and beverages available on school campuses during the school day and to set goals for nutrition education, physical activity, and other school-based activities designed to promote student wellness.

This chapter presents case studies of three promising innovations, one in each of the thematic areas. Each case study describes application of the SSA Method from the beginning stage of topic nomination, expert panel selection, and EA to the expert panel recommendations for future evaluation. In addition, each case study describes feedback and technical assistance provided to the innovation. The chapter concludes with a discussion about the aspects of EA that were most helpful in determining whether an environmental obesity prevention program or policy was ready for evaluation.

Food Access Case Study

The first case study describes the application of the SSA Method to the Pennsylvania Fresh Food Financing Initiative, which brings supermarkets to communities that lack access to healthy food.

The Pennsylvania Fresh Food Financing Initiative. The Food Trust is a nonprofit organization that stimulates creation of farmers' markets around Philadelphia. The Food Trust advocated for creation of the Pennsylvania Fresh Food Financing Initiative (FFFI) and manages it in partnership with the Reinvestment Fund (TRF) and the Greater Philadelphia Urban Affairs Coalition (GPUAC). FFFI aims to increase the number of supermarkets or grocery stores in underserved areas of Pennsylvania. FFFI serves the financing needs of potential supermarket operators in underserved communities where infrastructure costs and credit requirements cannot be fulfilled by conventional financial institutions.

The Food Trust, TRF, and the GPUAC all bring specific expertise to FFFI. The Food Trust works directly with the supermarket and grocery store industry, developers, and underserved communities to match appropriate projects to communities and lend support during the process of establishing or renovating a market. TRF is a community investment group with extensive experience lending to businesses in low-income neighborhoods by offering loan rates and terms that are more flexible and generous than those from commercial lenders. This flexibility includes loans that can be granted at various stages of development (e.g., predevelopment, acquisition), security interest (e.g., second mortgages, allowance for higher loan-to-capital ratios), and terms.

NEW DIRECTIONS FOR EVALUATION • DOI: 10.1002/ev

The GPUAC expands employment and contract opportunities for women and minorities among community projects, including hiring workers from surrounding communities and workforce development. Unemployment and lack of training have presented problems in many of the underserved neighborhoods where supermarkets are established; therefore FFFI focuses on community economic development by providing employment training and opportunities. Together, the Food Trust, the GPUAC, and TRF make grants for costs that operators are hesitant to incur without confidence that the store will be profitable.

FFFI opens new supermarkets and grocery stores in underserved communities and enables some supermarkets to renovate their refrigeration units and expand their stores, increasing the fresh food options available in low-income communities. In 2005, Philadelphia had the second lowest number of supermarkets per capita of major cities in the nation (Karpyn & Axler, 2006). By giving underserved people access to fresh food, greater variety of foods, and lower-priced food, FFFI hopes to add more nutritionally balanced options.

Setting Description. Stores eligible to apply and receive funds from FFFI must be located in low-to-moderate-income census tracts and in areas of below-average supermarket density. In Pennsylvania, funds are furnished to economically distressed areas, where (1) the unemployment rate is greater than 1.5 times the national average, (2) the poverty rate is greater than 20%, and (3) the median family income is less than 80% of the area median income. For metropolitan areas, the population must be greater than 1,500, and in a nonmetropolitan area, the population must be greater than 500. All stores funded through FFFI must agree to offer a full selection of fresh foods, including fruits and vegetables.

The Evaluability Assessment of FFFI. The evaluability assessment included a review of program documents, the development of a logic model, and a site visit involving interviews with key stakeholders.

How FFFI Was Selected. FFFI was nominated for an evaluability assessment by a researcher at Tulane University's Prevention Research Center because it was the nation's first statewide program aimed at increasing supermarket development in underserved areas. In addition, innovative financing for establishing and renovating supermarkets suggested that this program might be feasible in other low-income areas. Members of the Early Assessment initiative's expert panel expressed interest in exploring food access programs that were innovative, involved, had unique partnerships or coalitions, or were funded by using creative financing techniques. Members of the expert panel wanted to know where the funds came from, how they were distributed, and how innovative lending and financing could be used to promote development of supermarkets in low-income areas. In addition, the expert panel was interested in learning about the Food Trust's plan for replication in new communities and additional states.

NEW DIRECTIONS FOR EVALUATION • DOI: 10.1002/ev

Before the site visit, the EA team reviewed background materials about the innovation, including funding proposals, program reports, articles, brochures, presentations, and the website (Table 4.1). The document review helped to develop a draft logic model and served as a reference during analysis and report writing to clarify or give a more comprehensive context for the data collected throughout the evaluability assessment.

Table 4.1. Documents Reviewed for Fresh Food Financing Initiative (FFFI) Evaluability Assessment

Document	Comment
Supermarket Campaign Process Framework	The Food Trust's internal logic model for the FFFI
Pennsylvania's Fresh Food Financing Initiative: Case Study	A single-page case summary describing the goals and development of the FFFI
Food Geography: How Food Access Affects Diet and Health	A report detailing the connection between poor access to fresh foods and health outcomes
Fresh Food Financing Initiative v5	A PowerPoint presentation with an overview of the FFFI, from financing and partners to implementation and lessons learned
Closing the Grocery Gap in Underserved Communities: The Creation of the Pennsylvania Fresh Food Financing Initiative	Article by Food Trust staff submitted (and later accepted) for publication as Giang, T., Karpyn, A., Laurison, H., Hillier, A., & Perry, D. (2008). Closing the grocery gap in underserved communities: The creation of the Pennsylvania Fresh Food Financing Initiative. *Journal of Public Health Management and Practice*, 14(3), 272–279.
PA Power: Governor Rendell Announces Funding for Statewide Supermarket Initiative	September 2004 press release announcing partnership with TRF
SPECIAL REPORT: The Need for More Supermarkets in Philadelphia	Food Trust report sent to policy makers to spur creation of a task force
Supermarket Campaign—Programs and Initiatives—The Food Trust (http://www.the foodtrust.org/php/programs/super.market .campaign.php)	Webpage detailing the components of the Food Trust's Supermarket Campaign, including the FFFI
Supermarket Application for Eligibility	FFFI application form
Supermarket Application for Financing	FFFI application form

Site Visit. A two-person EA team visited FFFI in Philadelphia, November 13–15, 2007. The EA team conducted 12 interviews. Interview questions focused on these topics:

- The background and history of the initiative
- The description of financing for supermarkets
- Challenges and barriers to implementation of the initiative
- Strategies for addressing political and financial factors
- The reach to affect large numbers of the target population
- Partnerships
- Community awareness and involvement
- The data collection and evaluation plan
- Funding mechanisms
- Key insights for public health and prevention

During the first 2 days, the EA team interviewed a number of individuals:

- The Food Trust
  - Founder
  - Deputy director
  - Program manager
  - Director of research and evaluation (in a group interview)
  - Three program coordinators (group interview)
- The Reinvestment Fund
  - President and CEO
  - Director of special initiatives
- Six store owners and operators (group interview)
- Director of strategic initiatives, Greater Philadelphia Urban Affairs Coalition
- Chief of staff, Pennsylvania House of Representatives
- The Progress Investment Association (a community organization)
  - Chairman (group interview)
  - Secretary (group interview)
- A community member (teacher)

On the basis of documents in Table 4.1, the EA team prepared a draft logic model describing the links among program activities, outcomes, and goals before the site visit. The EA team revised the logic model, as they learned more about the program, by using interviews and observations during the site visit. On the final day, the EA team met with stakeholders to review and refine the logic model and discuss how program activities would lead to intended outcomes.

The EA team and program staff worked together to expand or clarify all components of the logic model. The group decided unanimously to divide the inputs into preprogram inputs, which were the influences or resources needed to get the FFFI funding passed by the state legislature, and program inputs, the resources needed for program implementation. The logic model was refined to ensure that each input had an associated activity or process, outputs, and outcomes. The EA team added processes as a category of inputs to reflect the fact that many of the activities were ongoing, iterative processes rather than single endeavors. The final logic model is seen in Figure 4.1.

Findings of the Evaluability Assessment. Evaluability assessment findings focus on the program's degree of implementation, plausibility, and feasibility.

Degree of Implementation. The first supermarket funded under FFFI, ShopRite of Island Avenue in Philadelphia, opened its doors September 20, 2004. The new 57,000 square foot supermarket created 258 jobs, and 54% of these employees lived in the neighborhood where the store was located.

Under the leadership of State Representative Dwight Evans, the state appropriated $30 million to FFFI, and an additional $90 million was leveraged by using a combination of public and private sources, including federal tax credits from the U.S. Treasury's New Markets Tax Credit Program. Since 2004, the initiative obtained and committed $38.9 million in grants and loans, established more than 50 supermarkets and grocery stores throughout Pennsylvania, created or preserved 3,723 jobs, and created 1.2 million square feet of food retail space.

According to the Food Trust staff and store operators, the success and profitability of FFFI-funded supermarkets has contradicted several supermarket industry assumptions that investment in low-income and inner-city areas has low returns. Interviews with community members indicated that the social environment changes when an FFFI-supported store opens in an underserved area. Local residents were pleased that they had a high-quality food outlet, and some communities used the stores (with the cooperation of the operator) as gathering places and centers for social services.

Plausibility. The logic model shows that FFFI is highly plausible as an intervention to improve health outcomes by reducing diet-related disease, increasing social capital, and improving community well-being. FFFI is based on empirical data suggesting that lack of access (caused by geographic, economic, structural, and other barriers) to fresh foods in communities leads to unhealthy eating patterns, which in turn lead to a higher rate of diet-related disease (Larson, Story, & Nelson, 2009; Moore, Diez Roux, Nettleton, & Jacobs, 2008). In addition, such inequities usually fall along racial, ethnic, and socioeconomic lines. FFFI addresses the determinants of unhealthy eating by opening stores that sell a variety of healthy foods at a low price point, which is believed to improve eating patterns in underserved communities. Further, the opening of new stores creates new jobs for community members, increasing workforce capacity, and contributing to community economic development.

NEW DIRECTIONS FOR EVALUATION • DOI: 10.1002/ev

Figure 4.1. Logic Model of the Fresh Food Financing Initiative

Philadelphia, PA

Problem statement: A healthy diet contributes to obesity prevention. Limited access to healthier food choices in terms of availability, affordability, and/or quality is a major barrier to maintaining a healthier diet among children in families with low incomes.

Pre-Program Inputs	Inputs	Activities/process	Outputs	Short-term outcomes	Intermediate outcomes	Long-term outcomes	Goals
Community need	Community need	Ongoing response to constituent need	Amount of funding to resource program	Increase in number of supermarkets opening and operating in underserved areas	Increased purchase and consumption of fresh produce and/or other healthier food options	Increased consumption of healthier food options	Contribute to improving the access to fresh foods
Political will and leadership (program champion)	Political will and leadership	Provision of technical assistance and human resources assistance to qualifying grantees and borrowers	# of applications for grants or loans	Revitalization of old stores and construction of new stores	Increased selection of fresh produce at markets in underserved areas	Ongoing construction of markets in underserved areas and maintenance of existing markets	Economic development
Establishment of evidence with background data collection	Public-private partnerships • The Reinvestment Fund (TRF) • The Food Trust (huge role)	• Food Trust • TRF • Others	# of grants and loans made	Increased access to (and increased variety of) affordable fresh produce and/or other healthier food options	Increased workforce capacity	Create jobs, revitalize commercial real estate, leverage private sector capital and increase tax ratables	Improved health outcomes due to: • Reduction in diet-related disease • Increased social capital • Improved well-being
• Educating decision-makers on findings		Outreach to promote program to communities and operators	# of stores constructed or renovated	Cost savings for community members • Lower food prices • Reduced transportation costs	Increased safety due to improved lighting, access, and security		
Task force representing a diversity of interests and committed to process • Health interests • University researchers • Dept. of public health (to offer evidence)	• The Greater Philadelphia Urban Affairs Coalition • Commonwealth of Pennsylvania	Determine eligible operators/locations	# of operators matched to communities	Jobs for community members	Increased development of other small enterprises • Supermarkets anchor developments for other retail	Provide lower cost, nutritious foods, and savings on transportation	
• Industry • Operators • Dept. of planning • Nonprofit civic groups	Process for funding grants and loans • Funding leveraged (new market tax credits)	Match communities to willing operators	# of new options for produce/healthier food	Supermarkets both meeting needs of consumers and meeting profitability objectives	Bundled health and social services in supermarkets • Other positive community outcomes/spinoffs	Promote a nutritionally balanced diet that leads to reduced rates of diet-related disease	
Advocate at state and local levels for funding, building relationships among community sectors	Financing or distribution mechanism to help establish or assist supermarkets in underserved areas • Grants • Debt financing	Land assembly (obtain space for construction of new supermarkets) Community commitment to deal with hurdles	# of jobs created	Greater food diversity	Increased knowledge of new healthy foods		
Financing and selective grant-making to reduce structural barriers							
Community buy-in							
Tax credits for economic development							

Financing legislation passed

| Data source to document accomplishment | Baseline data, data on activities to attain financing/distribution support data on grant and loan applications and outcomes Food Trust data collection | Food Trust data collection | Food Trust data collections | Food Trust data collection: data on additional grocers in low-income communities; store inventory and customer purchase data; labor statistics | Food Trust data collection: customer purchase data; loan and grant data; store inventory records; labor statistics; police records; tax records | Food Trust data collection: labor statistics; property assessments; tax records; census tract information; store inventories; morbidity and mortality data |

Contextual factors: Economic and market realities; balance of community involvement and project feasibility; level of political capital; organizational context (have to have partners available); surrounding community context (ethnic/racial mix; access to transportation); site control issues and politics (e.g., zoning and other regulations); importance of equally serving all constituents in state; state solvency; economic and market realities; level of political capital

Feasibility. At the time of the evaluability assessment, FFFI was fully implemented in the Philadelphia area and in several rural areas of Pennsylvania. Since 2004, 32 stores have opened, predominantly new stores in previously abandoned retail spaces. The Food Trust continues to receive applications from both store operators and community groups and works to match them to each other. Pennsylvania has increased funding because the program is viewed as successful.

Renovating or creating supermarkets and grocery stores requires extensive financial resources and community commitment. The Food Trust and TRF have worked to meet the financing needs of store owners who plan to operate in underserved communities, where infrastructure costs and credit needs cannot be filled solely by conventional financial institutions. FFFI is supported by strong public-private partnerships with a community development bank (TRF), an active community-based organization (GPUAC), champion state legislators, and funding leveraged from tax credits for economic development. By incorporating economic development into a public health intervention, this supermarket initiative secured millions of dollars in funding by bringing together legislators and public policy makers. Program staff members were able to demonstrate the broad benefits of the proposed initiative to nontraditional public health partners.

Recommendations for Evaluation. Research indicates that limited access to healthy food is associated with diet-related diseases. However, an association is not the same as demonstrating change: that how people access food will create a change in their diets and their risk for diet-related diseases. FFFI does not yet have evidence to demonstrate its effect on either health outcomes or individual dietary behavior. The Food Trust currently collects and analyzes these descriptive and process data:

- Number of applications received for funding
- Number of dollars awarded
- Number of stores constructed or opened in renovated spaces
- Square footage of food retail space created
- Total project costs for each project funded
- Sales figures before and after a project is funded
- Geographic distribution of stores
- Number of jobs created by a store opening

In addition, the Food Trust staff has compiled data from other sources, such as tax rates, labor statistics, census tract information, retail data, and morbidity and mortality data. This information has been used to assess the progress of implementation, economic impact of FFFI, and changing level of access to healthy foods in the state.

The Food Trust is very interested in conducting further evaluation of FFFI. Some areas for future evaluation are changes in individual shopping habits, eating behaviors, and consumer knowledge of nutrition before and after a store is established. Some stores may have a customer shopper or loyalty card that generates data about household purchasing patterns.

FFFI staff was encouraged to consider testing the logic model assumptions that when new supermarkets are established, fresh produce becomes available, affordable, and desirable, and customers purchase these foods. A tool such as the Nutrition Environment Measures Survey in Stores (NEMS-S) could be used to assess the availability and prices of healthier products in the new markets (Glanz, Sallis, Saelens, & Frank, 2007).

Even with good access to healthy foods, some customers may not choose to buy fresh fruits and vegetables. Because supermarkets carry both healthy and unhealthy food selections—and the FFFI has an explicit policy of noninterference with store inventory—there is no guarantee that individuals will make healthy choices. Several of the Food Trust's other initiatives have had a strong and well-received social marketing component. For example, the Food Trust's Snackin' Fresh social marketing campaign educates, engages, and energizes youth about healthy snack options. They have involved youths to help promote products by creating a video documenting their perspectives on available food choices in corner stores and why healthy eating is important. The FFFI may consider incorporating similar social marketing efforts into the program by adapting these components. Because the cost of food may still be a barrier for some residents, the FFFI could also consider adding a consumer education component to any social marketing materials and adding electronic benefit transfer systems (an electronic system that allows a recipient to authorize transfer of government benefits from a federal account to a retailer account to pay for products received).

Results of Second Expert Panel Review. The expert panel then reviewed the program after the evaluability assessment to make recommendations regarding evaluation.

Selection for Formal Evaluation. The expert panel members felt that FFFI is a strong program and one of the few that showed promise for a comprehensive, rigorous evaluation. Improved access to supermarkets may offer a powerful strategy to prevent childhood obesity. However, its effect on childhood obesity is less proximal than with programs providing direct services to children, such as child care. The panel recommended FFFI as one of the top priorities for a formal evaluation, recognizing that access to a supermarket would likely contribute to a healthy food environment, but that family practices and other contextual factors needed consideration as well.

The expert panel suggested multiple evaluation design possibilities, among them a prospective study as the initiative expands into other states, or a pre-and-post time-series analysis examining communities before, during, and after the store development and construction phase. A pre-post measure study or a longitudinal, multiple baseline study could be conducted by examining all the food outlets in the area where a new supermarket was proposed. Street intercept surveys, which survey people on the street,

Figure 4.2. How the Regression Discontinuity Design Might Be Applied to the Fresh Food Financing Initiative

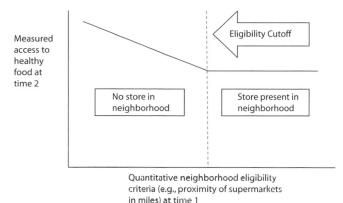

Measured access to healthy food at time 2

Eligibility Cutoff

No store in neighborhood

Store present in neighborhood

Quantitative neighborhood eligibility criteria (e.g., proximity of supermarkets in miles) at time 1

whether they are running errands, waiting for public transportation, or participating in recreational activities, can be used to understand the purchasing habits of a low-income, urban area.

A second possible evaluation design is regression discontinuity. By using a regression discontinuity design, the effect of opening a supermarket in an area where one did not previously exist could be estimated by demonstrating a discontinuity in the relationship between eligibility criteria and measured access. We would predict a flattening of the slope of the regression line; a store in the neighborhood means equal access to healthy food across neighborhoods (Figure 4.2).

A third suggestion compares supermarket interventions to those with farmers' markets in a cluster analysis and observes what differences the product selection, location, and seasonality of the markets made for their customers. Finally, an economic analysis could investigate whether there were any negative consequences for local small businesses.

Key Questions for Further Evaluation. The expert panel offered several key questions for further evaluation:

- How does FFFI bring grocery stores into low-income areas?
- How do programs involve community stakeholders in the supermarket development process?
- Does the presence of a supermarket in a low-income setting change the residents' eating behaviors?
- Are supermarkets the best (or only) way to get nutritious, fresh food to low-income populations?
- What other factors, besides availability, motivate people to use supermarkets to purchase healthy food options?

Child Care Setting Case Study

The second case study describes the application of the SSA Method to New York City's group day care regulations.

New York City Group Day Care Regulations. The New York City Department of Health and Mental Hygiene's (DOHMH) Bureau of Chronic Disease Prevention and Control developed regulations that help licensed group day care operators create an environment for young children that is conducive to healthier eating and age-appropriate physical activity. The regulations affect approximately 1,650 licensed group day care centers serving approximately 115,000 children. Day care centers range in size from fewer than 20 enrolled children to more than 100.

Description of Regulations. The New York City DOHMH passed legislation to amend Article 47 of the New York City Health Code on June 15, 2006, and this legislation became law on January 1, 2007 (Board of Health, 2008). DOHMH staff enforced the regulations through onsite inspections. The regulations stated the following:

- Children 12 months and older must have at least 60 minutes of physical activity, and among children 3 years and older, at least 30 of these 60 minutes must be structured activity.
- Children must have appropriate dress for outdoor play.
- Day care centers must have safe indoor play areas to continue physical activity even during inclement weather.
- Children shall receive no more than 6 ounces of 100% juice each day.
- Milk that is served to children over the age of 2 years will have a 1% fat content or less.
- Water must be readily available to children throughout the day.
- Sugar-sweetened beverages are prohibited.
- Day care centers must give parents nutrition guidelines for food brought into the center from outside.
- Television or video viewing of educational or physical fitness programming is limited to a maximum of 60 minutes each day only for children 2 years and older. Among children under the age of 2, television or video viewing is restricted.

Although not required by the regulations, DOHMH offered training and technical assistance to day care operators to meet the new requirements.

Setting Description. Densely populated, New York City has more than 8 million residents. Approximately 7% of the NYC population is under the age of 5, which equates to approximately 560,000 children. With more than half of these children in day care settings for as many as 8 hours a day, 5 days a week, an effective policy could have a substantial population-level impact.

The Evaluability Assessment of New York City's Day Care Regulations. The evaluability assessment included a review of regulation-related documents, the development of a logic model, and a site visit involving interviews with key stakeholders.

How the Day Care Regulations Were Selected for EA. The New York City DOHMH day care regulations, which were nominated by the deputy director of DOHMH's Bureau of Chronic Disease Prevention and Control, rose to the top of several nominated policies and programs in the after-school and day care thematic area. The specific questions the expert panel posed concerned how DOHMH conceived of the regulations and who conceived of them, how DOHMH proposed the regulations and presented them to city government, who the primary stakeholders were, and how DOHMH promoted the regulations and assisted their implementation. In addition, the expert panel wanted to know how DOHMH communicated to day care providers about the regulation changes, how DOHMH monitored and enforced the regulations, whether day care providers found the regulations acceptable and feasible, and how parents were involved. Lastly, the expert panel recommended that an impact evaluation of the regulations could include implementation data, behavior changes, body mass index, and parents as a potential source for data collection.

Site Visit. A two-person EA team visited New York City, October 9–11, 2007. Before the site visit, the EA team reviewed a number of documents to understand the regulations:

- New York City Department of Health and Mental Hygiene Board of Health Notice of Adoption of Amendments to Article 47 of the New York City Health Code
- New York City Department of Health and Mental Hygiene Change in New York City Health Child-Care Regulations
- New York City Department of Health and Mental Hygiene Part I: Summary of New Regulations on Nutrition for Group Child-Care Services Effective Date January 1, 2007
- New York City Department of Health and Mental Hygiene Part I: Summary of New Regulations on Physical Activity for Group Child-Care Services Effective Date January 1, 2007
- New York City Department of Health and Mental Hygiene NYC Vital Signs, Volume 5, No. 2. March 2006

The EA team conducted 12 in-depth interviews to gain understanding of the background, development, and implementation of the regulations. Interviews covered the background and history of the regulations, the outcomes that stakeholders hoped the regulations would achieve, day care staff training, awareness and compliance of the regulations, data collection activities, and the responses of children and parents. The EA team interviewed these stakeholders:

- DOHMH interviews
  - Bureau of Chronic Disease Prevention and Control

- Assistant commissioner, Bureau of Chronic Disease Prevention and Control
- Director, physical activity and nutrition
- Deputy director, physical activity and nutrition
- Program development specialist, physical activity and nutrition
- Training director, physical activity and nutrition
- Bureau of Child Care
  - Associate commissioner
  - Child care program director
- District Public Health Office
  - Two training outreach coordinators
  - Physical activity coordinator
- Day care operators
  - One local Head Start educational director
  - One local operator of a day care center

The EA team met with DOHMH administrators to discuss the logic model and preliminary findings on the last day of the site visit. The logic model discussion was brief because DOHMH administrators expressed interest in discussing programmatic knowledge and lessons from the field that the EA team could offer. The administrators also wanted to discuss potential evaluation questions and funding opportunities. DOHMH administrators and the EA team reviewed each section of the logic model. DOHMH offered suggestions for the logic model that the EA team then incorporated; however, the final logic model (seen in Figure 4.3) was quite similar to the original version.

Findings of the Evaluability Assessment. The evaluability assessment findings focus on the regulation's degree of implementation, plausibility, and feasibility.

Degree of Implementation. DOHMH's Bureaus of Child Care and Chronic Disease Prevention and Control jointly mailed materials that described the regulations to licensed group day care centers. DOHMH enforced the regulations through periodic inspections by sanitarians and visits by specialists from the Bureau of Child Care.

Even though the regulations did not require training and technical assistance, DOHMH provided this service to day care operators. For example, DOHMH offered training in the evidence-based SPARK (Sport, Play, & Active Recreation for Kids!) early childhood physical activity program (Sallis et al., 1997; SPARK, 2004). At the time of the site visit, DOHMH had given SPARK training to approximately 43% of day care centers affected by the regulations. DOHMH gave day care centers in the district office catchment areas additional coaching and onsite follow-up to implement SPARK. Other staff provided technical assistance through periodic inspections.

To address disparities in health outcomes, DOHMH established three district public health offices in areas of the city where negative health outcomes

Figure 4.3. Logic Model of Regulations for Day Care Settings in New York City

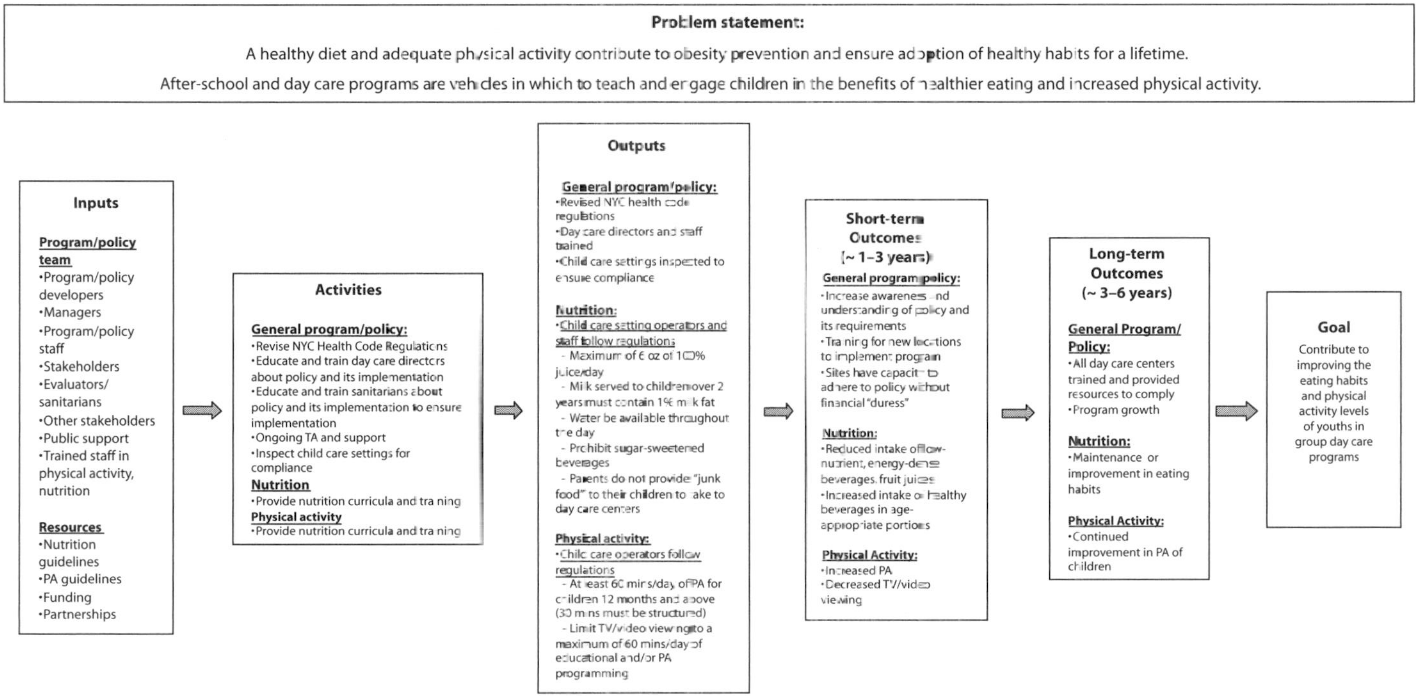

Problem statement:

A healthy diet and adequate physical activity contribute to obesity prevention and ensure adoption of healthy habits for a lifetime.

After-school and day care programs are vehicles in which to teach and engage children in the benefits of healthier eating and increased physical activity.

Inputs

Program/policy team
- Program/policy developers
- Managers
- Program/policy staff
- Stakeholders/
- Evaluators/
- sanitarians
- Other stakeholders
- Public support
- Trained staff in physical activity, nutrition

Resources
- Nutrition guidelines
- PA guidelines
- Funding
- Partnerships

Activities

General program/policy:
- Revise NYC Health Code Regulations
- Educate and train day care directors about policy and its implementation
- Educate and train sanitarians about policy and its implementation to ensure implementation
- Ongoing TA and support
- Inspect child care settings for compliance

Nutrition
- Provide nutrition curricula and training

Physical activity
- Provide nutrition curricula and training

Outputs

General program/policy:
- Revised NYC health code regulations
- Day care directors and staff trained
- Child care settings inspected to ensure compliance

Nutrition:
- Child care setting operators and staff follow regulations
  - Maximum of 6 oz of 100% juice/day
  - Milk served to children over 2 years must contain 1% milk fat
  - Water be available throughout the day
  - Prohibit sugar-sweetened beverages
  - Parents do not provide "junk food" to their children to take to day care centers

Physical activity:
- Child care operators follow regulations
  - At least 60 mins/day of PA for children 12 months and above (30 mins must be structured)
  - Limit TV/video viewing to a maximum of 60 mins/day of educational and/or PA programming

Short-term Outcomes (~1–3 years)

General program/policy:
- Increase awareness and understanding of policy and its requirements
- Training for new locations to implement program
- Sites have capacity to adhere to policy without financial "duress"

Nutrition:
- Reduced intake of low-nutrient, energy-dense beverages, fruit juices
- Increased intake of healthy beverages in age-appropriate portions

Physical Activity:
- Increased PA
- Decreased TV/video viewing

Long-term Outcomes (~3–6 years)

General Program/Policy:
- All day care centers trained and provided resources to comply
- Program growth

Nutrition:
- Maintenance or improvement in eating habits

Physical Activity:
- Continued improvement in PA of children

Goal

Contribute to improving the eating habits and physical activity levels of youths in group day care programs were most prevalent. The district offices furnished a variety of special services in these areas. For example, DOHMH trained day care operators in these areas in the state-funded Eat Well, Play Hard nutrition program, which targeted parents and children directly (New York State Department of Health, 2008).

Plausibility. Nutrition and physical activity guidelines may help promote healthy weight in children attending day care (Story, Kaphingst, & French, 2006). As indicated by the logic model, the regulations aimed to change the day care environment by providing nutrition and physical activity guidelines that day care staff and parents of enrolled children must follow. Researchers at New York University, with input from DOHMH, surveyed 40 group day care centers to understand current food service practices. Although fruits and vegetables, 100% juice, 1% milk, and whole wheat bread were served, unhealthy nutrition practices were also revealed. Examples included high-fat milk, less than 100% juice, and canned vegetables with high sodium content (Erinosho & Dixon, 2007).

Because the inputs, activities, and outputs outlined in the logic model are grounded in evidence, it is plausible the regulations can improve health outcomes related to poor diet and lack of physical activity in children enrolled in licensed group day care centers in New York City. For example, banning sugar-sweetened beverages on the premises will potentially lead to intended outcomes, such as children's reduced intake of sugar-sweetened beverages and increased intake of healthy beverages. Among toddlers, sugar-sweetened beverage consumption has increased and is related to the increased prevalence of childhood obesity (Dubois, Farmer, Girard, & Peterson, 2007; Fox, Reidy, Novak, & Ziegler, 2006). In addition, the physical activity outputs, providing 60 minutes of age-appropriate physical activity, and limiting television and video viewing times, contribute to the outcome of children's increased physical activity.

Levels of activity and television viewing have both been linked to obesity in young children (Mendoza, Zimmerman, & Christakis, 2007). Similarly, increasing physical activity to 60 minutes each day and reducing television time (for older children) have been found to reduce the prevalence of childhood obesity (Centers for Disease Control and Prevention, 1997; Epstein et al., 2008; Gortmaker et al., 1999; Robinson, 1999).

Feasibility. Implementation was feasible given the support from day care center operators and given that DOHMH provided day care center staff with training on the regulations.

Enforcement took place by using inspections and citations for violations, further increasing feasibility. Although DOHMH has not actually revoked a license, the threat of revocation is very powerful. Each day care center received an annual visit from a New York City DOHMH sanitarian and an early childhood educational consultant. These consultants ensured day care centers were following all regulations, in particular those for nutrition, physical activity, and television viewing. Consultants were former day care directors trained by DOHMH to support day care operators with implementation and compliance on nutrition and physical activity regulations. Thus consultants worked with day care operators on programming issues and ensured that lessons and play were age-appropriate. Both sanitarians and consultants have authority to cite day care operators if regulations are not being followed.

The regulations are generalizable to day care centers located in other cities and states, requiring only straightforward changes to improve nutrition, physical activity, and television viewing time. Other cities or states interested in replicating New York City's approach will likely need to train day care operators and staff about the importance of such regulations, obtain public support, offer programs to help meet the requirements, and develop an enforcement plan.

Recommendations for Evaluation. The New York City DOHMH expressed a strong interest in evaluation, and it was the focus of much discussion among the EA team. At the time of the site visit, the New York City DOHMH was collecting two kinds of data: the percentage of day care centers that had at least one staff member trained in SPARK, and questionnaires before and after participating in SPARK training that asked day care staff to report children's physical activity level. Data on training were limited because of high staff turnover. Specific evaluation questions of interest to New York City DOHMH administrators included:

- What kind of compliance data can be collected?
- How would these data be collected?
- Who would collect these data?
- How reliable would these data be?

There was consensus that data on compliance and enforcement would be useful for any future evaluation. In particular, administrators wanted to know how to measure compliance with the SPARK physical activity curriculum because data collectors could not directly observe compliance.

Results of the Second Expert Panel Review. The expert panel then reviewed the regulations after the evaluability assessment to make recommendations regarding evaluation.

Selection for Formal Evaluation. The expert panel was very enthusiastic in discussing New York City's day care regulations because of their extensive reach and inclusion of all racial and socioeconomic groups. The expert panel applauded the comprehensiveness of the regulations and their sustainability. The panel noted DOHMH's high level of interest in evaluation and its capacity for participating in evaluation. Therefore panel members singled out this policy as a high priority for evaluation, and indeed an evaluation funded by the Robert Wood Johnson Foundation and CDC began in 2009. In Phase I, 200 day care centers are sampled and classified as high- or low-implementing centers. The evaluation team will sample children from all these centers and collect data over 2 years on children's body mass index, physical activity, television viewing, and eating habits.

Key Questions for Further Evaluation. The expert panel offered these key questions for evaluation:

- Did inspection affect implementation of the regulations?
- How closely was adherence to the regulations monitored by city inspectors?
- Which day care centers were most likely to implement the regulations?
- What were the barriers and facilitators to implementation?
- What was the variation in implementation by site?
- What was the climate at day care centers? Were day care centers supportive or resistant to the regulations?
- What child-level outcomes could be collected?
- Could exposure to settings that adhered to the regulations help to prevent childhood obesity?
- What was the impact of the home environment as a means of support and influence on children's nutrition and physical activity?

School District Local Wellness Policy Case Study

The third case study describes the application of the SSA Method to the Natrona County School District's Local Wellness Policy.

Natrona County School District's Local Wellness Policy. Located in Casper, Wyoming, Natrona County School District No. 1 partnered with district and school staff, parents, and the community to implement the school district's local wellness policy. The policy's main goal was to improve the nutrition and physical activity behaviors of Natrona County prekindergarten through 12th-grade students.

Policy Description. The Natrona County school district's local wellness policy (NCLWP) established goals for nutrition, physical activity, and other school-based activities. The district outlined four overall goals in its policy:

- To offer food of good nutritional content on a typical school day
- To offer sequential, interdisciplinary, comprehensive, standards-based curriculum for lifelong physical activity and nutrition choices
- To create an environment that sends consistent wellness messages
- To establish a monitoring system for policy activities

Through administrative regulations and specific nutrition guidelines, the district provided additional guidance on how each goal was to be accomplished. The specific objectives of the NCLWP were:

- Establish health bars offering fruit and vegetables.
- Remove sodas and other beverages with high sugar content from vending machines.

- Establish school-based activities focused on nutrition and physical activity.
- Establish alternative fundraising that does not rely on junk food sales, and use approaches to student behavior management that do not rely on food as a reward or physical activity as a punishment.
- Train classroom and physical education faculty on nutrition and physical activity curriculum.
- Establish parent education programs.

Setting Description. Natrona County School District No. 1 is a large, rural school district in Casper, Wyoming. During the 2007–08 school year, the school district consisted of 38 public schools (pre-K through 12th grade) with approximately 11,601 students (Natrona County School District, 2007). Thirty-three percent of students in the district were eligible for the free or reduced-price lunch program.

Evaluability Assessment of Local Wellness Policy. The evaluability assessment included a review of policy documents, the development of a logic model, and a site visit involving interviews with key stakeholders.

How the Policy Was Selected. The school district's Physical Education Coordinator nominated NCLWP for consideration. The expert panel selected NCLWP because it included innovative strategies to promote healthy eating and physical activity; it was implemented in a large, rural school district; it used a phased approach to implementing the policy; and its implementation was strongly supported by the school district. In particular, the expert panel members were impressed by the strategies used to facilitate implementation and sustainability. For example, the district hired a full-time, district-level, school health coordinator to oversee policy implementation, appropriated a total of $57,500 to facilitate implementation, and encouraged schools to identify school level wellness representatives. In addition, the district used healthy school projects as a way to encourage schools to promote nutrition and physical activity to best meet their needs. The expert panel recognized that many school districts might not have sufficient funding to implement a local wellness policy as Natrona County did, but they felt it was important to determine whether such a large investment would result in a substantial return.

Site Visit. A two-person EA team visited Casper, October 2–4, 2007. Here is a list of documents reviewed as part of the EA:

- Action for Healthy Kids Information Packet
- Natrona County Local Wellness Policy
- Natrona County District School Survey
- Increased Funding Request

- Student Wellness Policy Healthy School Projects Action Plan Regulations
- Healthy School Project Action Plan (sample)
- School Vending Report
- Physical Education Standards
- Natrona County School District Enrollment by Grade

Prior to the site visit, the EA team drafted a logic model on the basis of a document review and phone conversations with the school health coordinator. The EA team conducted a total of 13 individual interviews with staff of the district:

- District school health coordinator
- Five District School Advisory Committee members
- School nurse (elementary school)
- Three school principals (elementary and junior high school)
- Physical educator (elementary school)
- Wellness site representative (junior high school)
- Teacher (junior high school)

During the site visit, the EA team visited an elementary school and two junior high schools to observe implementation of changes in the school environment. The team observed vending machines, lunch service, gymnasiums, and physical education classes.

On the final day of the visit, the EA team met with key stakeholders to review and modify the logic model. The goals were clearly articulated in various policy materials and elicited little discussion, but there was extensive discussion regarding the activities, outputs, and outcomes of the policy implementation. The stakeholders agreed with the activities as listed by the EA team, but they made several additions. Much of the discussion centered on establishing outcomes. Stakeholders were willing to establish measures for the various policy components, but in the absence of baseline data they were not comfortable identifying numerical targets for improvement, increased policy implementation, or impact. The EA team proposed general outcomes, which the stakeholders then clarified. The EA team encouraged the stakeholders to revisit the logic model and update the specific measures once a starting point for measurement had been established (Figure 4.4).

The EA team also offered both programmatic and evaluation technical assistance. Programmatic recommendations focused on:

- Working more closely with parents to engage them in the process of policy implementation
- Increasing and sustaining community involvement in implementation
- Suggesting resources to increase provision of nutrition education and for fundraising by using nonfood items

NEW DIRECTIONS FOR EVALUATION • DOI: 10.1002/ev

Figure 4.4. Logic Model of Natrona County School District's Local Wellness Policy

Natrona County School District, Casper, Wyoming

Problem statement: The physical activity and nutritional habits of Natrona County students are in need of improvement.

Overall policy goals: 1) To offer foods of good nutritional content or typical school day; 2) To offer sequential, interdisciplinary, comprehensive standards-based curriculum for life-long physical activity and nutrition decision's among students; 3) To create an environment that provides consistent wellness messages, is conducive to healthy choices, and contributes to forming life-long habits; and 4) To establish/use a DSWAC to help monitor HSP implementation.

Inputs

District student wellness advisory committee (DSWAC) members

Certified and classified staff/employees

Community members

PCAC (parent community advisory council)

Student wellness site representatives

Policy
-Local wellness policy adopted 5/22/06
-Employee wellness policy adopted 1991

Resources:

USDA federal guidelines—nutrition
Wyoming action for healthy kids
Western dairy council

NASPE guidelines
- Physical activity
Wyoming Action for Healthy Kids

PEP grant

Survey

Curriculum and instruction committee

Activities

District policies and support

1a Purchase health bars for elementary schools [s.smX]
1b Allocate money for vending machine revenue loss
1c Develop food list for snacks, fundraising, parties
1d Provide initial purchase costs for health bars

3a Provide training inservice to principals on approved policy and regulations (fall 06)
3b Identify coordinator of student wellness and provide support of position (summer 06)
3c Design district student wellness website
3d Identify alternatives to withholding physical activity for behavioral issues (fall 06)
3e Develop a list of alternative fundraising ideas
3f Develop protocol for health school projects (HSP)
3g Create opportunities for community-based activity
3i Promote policy concepts to parent/community
3j Promote policy concepts to staff/employees

4a Provide incentive for policy and regulation changes at each school (summer 06/07)
4b Assist with HSPs report development and submission to DSWAC
4c Submit monthly activity (web-based) report to the Curriculum and Instruction subcommittee of the school board
4d Discuss alternatives for evaluation of components

School practices & environment

1a Implement health bars and healthy food alternatives to students
1b Review/apply provided food list when needed
2a Use curriculum to promote life-long physical activity and nutrition

3a Provide trainings to select groups of employees on policy and regulations
3b Develop alternative plans for fundraising
3c Identify school wellness representative staff/employee
3d Promote policy concepts to staff/employee
3e Inform parents about policy and regulations
3f Develop/implement projects/annually involving
3i Promote healthy lifestyle—HSPs
4b Submit annual HSP report to DSWAC using assistance from DSWAC members

Outputs

District policies & support

1a # / schools received health bars (1—2 bars per school, depending on enrollment)
1b Total amount of compensation for vending machine—$30,000 Total estimated loss only promoted by one school
1c List of foods used for snacks, fundraising, parties has been created
1d Provided ~$100,000 for initial purchase of bars and supplies

3a ~75-80% of schools have received in-service training
3b Identified Coordinator and established an ongoing budget item
3c Completed 'website' 2 pages
3d List of alternatives for behavior issues
3e List of alternative fundraising ideas has been created
3f ___ schools have developed HSP
3g Activities in 2007-2008 school year (e.g., walks)
3i/3j Newsletters, flyers, meetings; training materials for unhealthy choices)
3j # of how school leaders, staff and community members

3i Total amount of support and type of acknowledgement for HSP teams—$27,500

4a $4.5C per student/school
4b DSWAC has provided assistance to all for submission of HSPs
4c Reports developed and submitted

School practices and environment

1a Utilize all health bars provided by the district—have introduced variety of lunch options to students
2a 1 schools currently uses health curriculum—body work: 1 elementary school uses a combination of PE curricula
3a 75-90% of schools have received training on PE schedule
3b 44% schools have submitted 3 HSPs/school
3f 50% of schools have submitted alternative fundraising items
3c 3 of 34 schools have wellness representatives
3c/3i New letters, flyers, PTO and faculty development meetings and other media have been used to promote policy
4b 54% of schools have submitted HSPs to DSWAC

Short-term Outcomes (~1–3 years) by 2010

District policies & support

1 Increase # and number of healthier food choices in school during the school day by 90%
1 Sustain 'number of health bars in the elementary schools
1 Increase number of alternative / healthier snacks, party, and snack options by 10% annually
1 Increase funding to maintain choices available on health bars by 1% annually
3 Establish number of parents and other community members who are aware of and understand policies
3 Establish % of community member representation at least once at DSWAC meetings
3 Improve number of schools who have developed/submitted HSP
3 Establish use of alternative choices for fun/raising activities while maintaining items# unhealthy choices)
3 Vary type of activities provided/annually
DSWAC members will assist in the discussion of wellness activities with C and I subcommittee
3 Increase awareness and understand % of policy concepts (by staff, strong leaders, staff and community members
3 Increase activities with employee member to promote health behaviors
3 Establish and maintain ___ (# of resources used to sustain partnerships with groups (PCAC) to complete these tasks

School practices and environment

1 Increase number of healthier food choices in schools during the school day by 80%
1 Sustain 'number of health bar in each school
1 Increased number of alternative/ healthier snacks, party, and snack options by 10% annually
+ Additional snacks (# will adopt and implement a nutrition curriculum
1 Every teacher will have an understanding of the concepts related to the policy (how and why
1 Increase activities to promote life-long choices by
1 Establish number of staff trained on policy components at each school
1 Establish use of alternative choices for 'unc raising of alternative fundraising items,# unhealthy choices)
+ Increase number of schools who have developed/submitted HSP

Intermediate outcomes (~1–3 years)

1 Increased number of healthier food choices in schools during the school day by 90%
1 Sustain number of health bars in the elementary schools
1 Increased use of alternative choices (by 10%) for fundraising, party, and snack options
1 Maintain increased funding for choices available on health bars by 10% annually

3 Every teacher will have an understanding of the concepts related to the policy (how and why
3 Partner with employee wellness to promote health behaviors
3 Increase the number of resources used to promote policy components (monthly, annually); sustain partnerships with groups (PCAC) to complete these tasks
3 Increase the number of students served by the HSPs
3 Increased parent and community involvement in all district wellness activities
3 Improve number of schools who have developed/submitted HSP
3 Increase number and variety of alternative choices for fundraising (# alternative fundraising items,# unhealthy choices)
4 Sustain relationship between DSWAC and school members to implement and monitor policy components

Long-term outcomes (~4–6 years)

1 Increased number of healthier food choices in schools during the school day by 100%
1 Sustain number of health bars in the elementary schools
1 Increased number of alternative/ healthier fundraising, party, and snack options by 10% annually
1 Maintain increased funding for choices available on health bars by 10% annually
2 Every teacher will have an understanding of the concepts related to the policy (how and why)
2 Increase number of activities completed by partnering with other wellness initiatives
2 Increase and update resources used to promote policy components (monthly, annually); sustain partnerships with groups (PCAC) to complete these tasks
2 Increase the number of students served by the HSPs; sustain existing level of funding for HSPs
2 Increase numbers of parents and other community members who are aware of and understand policies and involved in policy implementation
3 Improve number of schools who have developed/submitted HSP
3 Increase number and variety of alternative choices for fundraising (# alternative fundraising items/# unhealthy choices)
4 Sustain relationship between DSWAC and school members to implement, monitor and modify policy

Milestones

Milestones: identify individuals to partner on evaluation of policy; establish evaluation protocol to measure policy components

Milestones: Continue to evaluate outcome measures and modify policy components accordingly

Data source to document accomplishment

Contextual factors

Health school projection plan (form, vend ing purchase documents, contracts, profit statements, vending items costs, annual dietitian logs, enrollment form, classified fitness, information)

Leadership; Socioeconomic status; school culture

- Conducting an analysis of future curricula for health and physical education (Centers for Disease Control and Prevention, 2006, 2007)

Findings of the Evaluability Assessment. The evaluability assessment findings focus on the policy's degree of implementation, plausibility, and feasibility.

Degree of Implementation. During the first year of implementation, Natrona County School District No. 1 improved offerings of foods of good nutritional value. Specifically, they focused on eliminating sodas and other drinks with high sugar content from the vending machines during school hours, improving the quality of foods offered to students, and installing health bars for schools.

The school district also promoted consistent, healthful messages and opportunities for physical activity and education by using healthy school projects. At the time of the site visit, 50% of schools had submitted documentation of their healthy school projects for the school year. The district also encouraged physical activity outside of school through activities such as community walking events. The nutrition curriculum was under development and was to be implemented in the second year. The district also created and was distributing a resource binder for all physical education teachers, containing information on physical activity, equipment, and assessment. The district designated physical education as an area of focus in the second year. Finally, the district school wellness advisory committee was charged with monitoring implementation. They planned to collaborate with the district's assessment department, which normally conducts student testing and evaluation, to determine how best to monitor policy implementation.

Plausibility. As the logic model delineates, full implementation of the NCLWP made it a highly plausible approach to improve the physical activity and nutrition habits of Natrona County students. The literature on healthy school environments suggests that activities like those outlined in the logic model will ultimately contribute to reducing childhood obesity in this population (Wechsler et al., 2004). The policy targeted two of the primary determinants of childhood obesity: poor nutritional habits and physical inactivity.

Feasibility. Several factors made full implementation of the NCLWP feasible. First was the district's commitment to implementation of the local wellness policy through provision of financial resources. An annual budget of $57,500 for implementation of the local wellness policy made it feasible for the policy to be implemented and ensured sustainability. Funds were used to:

- Offset the revenue losses from vending machine changes
- Support a school health coordinator position
- Support healthy school projects
- Supplement nutritional provisions for school lunches and snacks
- Foster incentives for schools to carry out their healthy school projects

Second, the district created a dedicated staff position to oversee implementation of the local wellness policy, communicate regularly with schools regarding policy implementation, and coordinate the district school wellness advisory committee. Third, phased implementation of the NCLWP allowed various activities of the policy to be accomplished over time, making it less burdensome to implement and assess. Fourth, flexibility of policy implementation, which instilled a sense of ownership among school personnel, was a factor. Fifth, the district had a fully functioning district school wellness advisory committee that met regularly and offered guidance related to policy implementation. Finally, the district implemented a variety of low-cost strategies to aid implementation; as an example, the district used a mix of canned and fresh fruits and vegetables and increased the price of the school meal by 10 cents to offset the cost of these offerings.

Recommendations for Evaluation. Evaluation is an important component of the federally mandated local wellness policies. Having completed only one year of implementation, the Natrona County School District No.1 has conducted very little evaluation. Stakeholders expressed a need to identify an evaluation consultant and furnish funding for evaluating the policy components and the implementation process.

The district conducted annual health assessments on elementary school students and collected health risk behavior data using the Youth Risk Behavior Survey from high school students (Eaton et al., 2008) and student fitness data by using FitnessGram (Welk & Meredith, 2008). The EA team noted that although these data were collected, they were not coordinated or compared analytically to determine the impact of the policy on student behaviors. In general, surveys are conducted independently and results are analyzed and reported independently. Very little information had been extracted from these data sources to assess the impact of the policy after one year of implementation.

The EA team and CDC experts recommended use of a systematic process evaluation to document the degree to which schools were implementing the policy, and to identify schools that were having difficulty implementing policy components. Those schools could then get help and guidance from the district. A formal evaluation plan is needed that clearly outlines who will conduct the evaluation, what will be evaluated, what types of data sources will be used for evaluation, how the evaluation will be conducted, and timelines for evaluation.

Results of Second Expert Panel Review. The expert panel then reviewed the policy after the evaluability assessment to make recommendations regarding evaluation.

Selection for Formal Evaluation. Expert panel members agreed that the NCLWP had the potential to improve the schools' food and fitness environment significantly, affect positive changes in students' eating and physical activity, and contribute to reducing the prevalence of obesity and overweight. Expert panel members felt strongly that the NCLWP was a well-written policy and one that could be fully implemented. They believed further investigation of the policy would yield insights about what was required to implement the policy successfully and detect changes in the nutrition and physical activity of the nation's youth. The expert panel recognized the difficulty school districts faced in developing and implementing strong local wellness policies, and they recommended a cluster evaluation of such policies by using a series of case studies.

The expert panel believed that, on the whole, few local wellness policies were fully implemented. Yet because local wellness policies were federally mandated, the field would benefit and learn from a process evaluation of the NCLWP. A process evaluation would document and analyze the development and implementation of the policy, assessing whether strategies were implemented as planned and whether expected outputs were produced. Differential implementation of the policy across the district was also a potential opportunity for a comparison study. The NCLWP was recommended for a formal evaluation. Potential funding agencies are interested in evaluating the NCLWP.

Key Questions for Further Evaluation. The expert panelists asked five key evaluation questions:

Is federal legislation requiring local wellness policies unrealistic?
Are local wellness policies being implemented?
In places where the local wellness policies are being implemented, how were they developed and implemented?
What are the characteristics of a school district that can successfully implement a local wellness policy?
What are the outcomes?

Conclusion

Benefits and Challenges of EA and the SSA Method. These case studies illustrate how the SSA Method, and specifically the evaluability assessments at its core, gives evaluators the opportunity to examine the reality of an innovation and determine its plausibility, feasibility, and readiness for evaluation. Several themes emerged from these evaluability assessments that illustrate the benefits and challenges of the approach.

Input from Stakeholders. An important part of EA is to consult with a broad and diverse group of stakeholders. They can bring varying perspectives to help EA teams understand what these policies and programs have accomplished and how they came to be. However, it is sometimes a challenge to identify a broad and diverse set of stakeholders. Inspection of the interviews in our three case studies indicates that it was not a perfect process because the EA teams had to select stakeholders from a distance. However, stakeholder input in all three cases strengthened the case for further evaluation.

A Transparent Process Puts Stakeholders at Ease. Discussions about evaluation can be intimidating for program staff. For this reason, it was vital to clarify the purpose of evaluability assessment for learning about programs and policies. EA is not evaluation; it solicits input from the staff, and they realize there is something to be gained by their participation.

Logic Models. The development of the logic model is critically important in delineating program or policy components, activities, and outcomes. The logic model served as a tool to create dialog with stakeholders about their innovation, ensure there was accurate understanding of the programs, and be the basis for discussion of evaluation with stakeholders.

Constructive Feedback and Technical Assistance. The EA process and the follow-on technical assistance by CDC experts offered something of value to stakeholders to reciprocate the time and attention they gave to the Early Assessment initiative. With a few exceptions (Leviton et al., in press; Smith, 1989) this advantage of EA has gone largely unrecognized in the evaluation literature. Stakeholders felt energized about improving their program or policy implementation on the basis of the recommendations and resources from the EA teams. In some cases, they became more confident about collecting data, or about using current data to monitor their program, or identifying an evaluator.

Expert Panel Input. The panel's expertise was critical in making judgments about plausibility, feasibility, and readiness for evaluation on the basis of the limited information that an EA could furnish. The expertise of the panel also proved critical in determining evaluation designs and questions.

What Comes Next? Plans for Formal Evaluation

The Early Assessment initiative produced a report to potential funders of evaluation in hopes of securing their interest in these innovations. Evaluation of the New York City day care regulations is under way as of this writing. The FFFI is a topic of active discussion among federal policy makers, and it is likely to undergo outcome evaluation within the near future once it is replicated in several states. The Natrona County school district's local wellness policy may become part of a cluster evaluation, provided that a funder can be attracted to such a project.

In sum, the three cases presented in this chapter show how promising and potentially effective approaches to addressing childhood obesity can be identified by using a systematic process. Formal evaluation of these initiatives in the community, child care, and school environments will be a step in successfully addressing healthier eating and physical activity, moving us in the right direction to reverse the U.S. epidemic of childhood obesity.

References

Board of Health. (2008). *Notice of adoption of the repeal and reenactment of Article 47 of the New York City Health Code*. Retrieved September 8, 2009, from http://www.nyc.gov/html/doh/downloads/pdf/public/notice-adoption-hc-art47-0308.pdf

Centers for Disease Control and Prevention. (1997). Guidelines for school and community programs to promote lifelong physical activity among young people. *Morbidity and Mortality Weekly Report, 46* (no. RR-6), 1–36.

Centers for Disease Control and Prevention. (2006). *Physical Education Curriculum Analysis Tool*. Atlanta: Author.

Centers for Disease Control and Prevention. (2007). *Health Education Curriculum Analysis Tool*. Atlanta: Author.

Child Nutrition and WIC Reauthorization Act of 2004. (2004). Public Law No. 108-265, 118 Stat 729. Retrieved September 8, 2009, from http://www.fns.usda.gov/cnd/Governance/Legislation/Historical/PL_108-265.pdf

Dubois, L., Farmer, A., Girard, M., & Peterson, K. (2007). Regular sugar-sweetened beverage consumption between meals increases risk of overweight among preschool-aged children. *Journal of the American Dietetic Association, 107*, 924–934.

Eaton, D., Kann, L., Kinchen, S., Shanklin, S., Ross, J., Hawkins, J., et al. (2008). Youth Risk Behavior Surveillance—United States, 2007. *Morbidity and Mortality Weekly Report, 57*(no. SS-4), 1–131.

Epstein, L. H., Roemmich, J. N., Robinson, J. L., Paluch, R. A., Winiewicz, D. D., Fuerch, J. H., et al. (2008). A randomized trial of the effects of reducing television viewing and computer use on body mass index in young children. *Archives of Pediatrics and Adolescent Medicine, 162*, 239–245.

Erinosho, T., & Dixon, L. B. (2007). Involvement of nutrition and dietetic students in a community-based research project. *Topics in Clinical Nutrition, 22*, 367–377.

Fox, M. K., Reidy, K., Novak, T., & Ziegler, P. (2006). Sources of energy and nutrients in the diets of infants and toddlers. *Journal of the American Dietetic Association, 106*, S28–S42.

Glanz, K., Sallis, J. F., Saelens, B. E., & Frank, L. D. (2007). Nutrition Environment Measures Survey in Stores (NEMS-S): Development and evaluation. *American Journal of Preventive Medicine, 32*(4), 282–289.

Gortmaker, S. L., Peterson, K., Wiecha, J., Sobol, A. M., Dixit, S., Fox, M. K., et al. (1999). Reducing obesity via a school-based interdisciplinary intervention among youth: Planet Health. *Archives of Pediatric and Adolescent Medicine, 153*(4), 409–418.

Karpyn, A., & Axler, F. (2006). *Food Geography: How Food Access Affects Diet and Health*. The Food Trust and the Philadelphia Health Management Corporation. Retrieved September 9, 2009, from http://www.thefoodtrust.org/pdf/Food%20Geography%20Final.pdf

Larson, N. I., Story, M. T., & Nelson, M. C. (2009). Neighborhood environments: Disparities in access to healthy foods in the U.S. *American Journal of Preventive Medicine, 36*(1), 74–81.

Leviton, L. C., Kettel Khan, L., Rog, D., Dawkins, N., & Cotton, D. (in press). Evaluability assessment to improve public health. *Annual Review of Public Health*.

Mendoza, J. A., Zimmerman, F. J., & Christakis, D. A. (2007). Television viewing, computer use, obesity, and adiposity in U.S. preschool children. *International Journal of Behavioral Nutrition and Physical Activity, 4*, 44.

Moore, L. V., Diez Roux, A. V., Nettleton, J. A., & Jacobs, D. R., Jr. (2008). Associations of the local food environment with diet quality: A comparison of assessments based on surveys and geographic information systems. The multi-ethnic study of atherosclerosis. *American Journal of Epidemiology, 167*(8), 917–924.

Natrona County School District. (2007). *Natrona County School District No. 1.* Retrieved September 8, 2009, from www.greatschools.net/cgi-bin/wy/district_profile/40?schoolID = 240

New York State Department of Health. (2008). *Eat well, play hard in child care settings curriculum.* Albany: Author.

Ogden, C. L., Carroll, M. D., & Flegal, K. M. (2008). High body mass index for age among U.S. children and adolescents, 2003–2006. *JAMA, 299,* 2401–2405.

Robinson, T. N. (1999). Reducing children's television viewing to prevent obesity: A randomized controlled trial. *Journal of the American Medical Association, 282*(16), 1561–1567.

Sallis, J. F., McKenzie, T. L., Alcaraz, J. E., Kolody, B., Faucette, N., & Hovell, M. F. (1997). The effects of a 2-year physical education program (SPARK) on physical activity and fitness in elementary school students. *American Journal of Public Health, 87,* 1328–1334.

Smith, M. F. 1989. *Evaluability assessment: A practical approach.* Boston: Kluwer Academic.

SPARK. (2004). The SPARK Early Childhood Physical Activity Program. Retrieved September 8, 2009, from http://www.sparkpe.org/programEarlyChildhood.jsp

Story, M., Kaphingst, K. M., & French, S. (2006). The role of child care settings in obesity prevention. *The Future of Children, 16,* 143–168.

Wechsler, H., McKenna, M. L., Lee, S. M., & Deitz, W. H. (2004). The role of schools in preventing childhood obesity: Childhood obesity. *State Education Standard,* 4–12.

Welk, G. J., & Meredith, M. D. (Eds.). (2008). *Fitnessgram/Activitygram reference guide.* Dallas: Cooper Institute.

Wholey, J. S. (2004). Evaluability assessment. In J. S. Wholey, H. P. Hatry, & K. E. Newcomer, *Handbook of practical program evaluation* (pp. 33–62). San Francisco: Jossey-Bass.

SERAPHINE PITT BARNES *is a Health Scientist in the Division of Adolescent and School Health at the Centers for Disease Control and Prevention (CDC).*

HOLLY WETHINGTON *is a Behavioral Scientist on the Research and Surveillance Team in the Division of Nutrition, Physical Activity, and Obesity at the Centers for Disease Control and Prevention (CDC).*

KAREN CHEUNG *is a Research Manager at ICF Macro.*

Kettel Khan, L., Dawkins, N., & Leviton, L. C. (2010). Impact, insights, and implications of the Systematic Screening and Assessment Method. In L. C. Leviton, L. Kettel Khan, & N. Dawkins (Eds.), *The Systematic Screening and Assessment Method: Finding innovations worth evaluating. New Directions for Evaluation, 125,* 95–110.

5

Impact, Insights, and Implications of the Systematic Screening and Assessment Method

Laura Kettel Khan, Nicola Dawkins, Laura C. Leviton

Abstract

The authors present both impressions and evidence about early impacts of the Systematic Screening and Assessment (SSA) Method as applied to childhood obesity prevention. They describe how the approach has rapidly identified policy and environmental interventions that are promising and worthy of further study, contributed to field knowledge about childhood obesity prevention, and encouraged further development of specific policies and environmental interventions. The SSA Method presents a new way of identifying promising interventions from the field. By stimulating discussion of real-world application among prevention researchers, it has contributed to developing a research agenda for policy and environmental approaches to prevention. By identifying real-world applications for formal evaluation, SSA facilitates a process parallel to translation of research to practice: that is, translation of practice to research. © Wiley Periodicals, Inc., and the American Evaluation Association.

Note: The findings and conclusions presented are those of the authors and do not necessarily represent the official position of the agencies.

Early Assessment of Programs and Policies to Prevent Childhood Obesity was a 2-year initiative to identify, screen, and assess community programs and policies to prevent childhood obesity. The initiative focused on policy and environmental interventions aimed at improving the diet and physical activity of children. The project was funded by a grant from the Robert Wood Johnson Foundation (RWJF) to the National Foundation for the Centers for Disease Control and Prevention (CDC). The initiative was implemented by three separate divisions of the CDC National Center for Chronic Disease Prevention and Health Promotion: the Division of Nutrition, Physical Activity and Obesity (DNPAO); the Division of Adolescent and School Health (DASH); and the Prevention Research Centers Program Office of the Division of Adult and Community Health. ICF Macro served as the coordinating center for the initiative. The Early Assessment initiative employed the Systematic Screening and Assessment (SSA) Method, of which it is the first test and example. As used in the Early Assessment initiative, the SSA Method was a systematic nomination and selection process to identify and screen a high volume of real-world policy and environmental interventions that are potentially effective in preventing childhood obesity.

This chapter is about how the initiative—both process and findings—has influenced a variety of audiences. There is evidence that the individual evaluability assessments were useful to the developers of these policies and programs. Also, cross-site knowledge has emerged for each of the five content areas that were investigated, as reported in the five synthesis documents. In addition, however, the initiative permitted important insights for the field of community-based obesity prevention, for research on prevention programs in general, and for further development of the method itself. The SSA Method is unique not only in the field of community-based obesity prevention but as a process to discover promising real-world interventions in general. As such, it is arguably a useful addition to evaluation methods more generally.

The SSA Method identifies and screens a high volume of real-world interventions to select those that are both ready for evaluation and highly promising in terms of their plausible effectiveness, reach into the target population, feasibility, and generalizability. The process includes six steps: selecting the content areas for study, obtaining a high volume of nominations of interventions, screening of the nominations by a panel of content experts and evaluators to select those worthy of further study, conducting evaluability assessments of the selected interventions, convening a second meeting of the panel to determine the priority of the interventions to undergo formal evaluation, and using the information. The information can be employed in three ways: to position the most promising interventions for formal evaluation, to provide feedback and technical assistance to the intervention developers and managers, and to create a synthesis report in each content area studied.

NEW DIRECTIONS FOR EVALUATION • DOI: 10.1002/ev

Over 2 years, five content areas for childhood obesity prevention were chosen, including access to healthy foods in low-income communities, day care and after-school environments, school district local wellness policies, comprehensive school physical activity programs, and interventions on the built environment to encourage physical activity. The initiative obtained 458 nominations; 174 of them met inclusion criteria, 48 underwent evaluability assessments, and 20 interventions on childhood obesity were determined to be both highly promising and ready for evaluation. We used the information to develop an agenda for evaluation that will focus future evaluation resources on the most promising policies and programs. In addition, the initiative provided feedback and technical assistance to the 48 intervention developers, and it developed synthesis reports in the five content areas under study (Cheung, Dawkins, Kettel Khan, & Leviton, 2009; Pitt Barnes, Robin, Dawkins, Leviton, & Kettel Khan, 2009a, 2009b; Skelton, Dawkins, Leviton, & Kettel Khan, 2009; Wethington, Hall, Dawkins, Leviton, & Kettel Khan, 2009). This chapter concerns the impact of these products and of the process itself.

Impacts on Obesity Prevention Efforts

A New Focus on Policy and Environmental Interventions. Policy and environmental interventions were selected for study because very few behavioral interventions have been effective to date in preventing obesity, and one-on-one behavioral interventions do not have enough reach into the population of children at risk to have an impact on national prevalence (Glasgow, Vogt, & Boles, 1999; Koplan, Liverman, & Kraak, 2005). Policy and environmental interventions demonstrated their effectiveness in tobacco control; a tax on tobacco discourages youths from initiating smoking, and laws and ordinances for smoke-free businesses increase the number of smokers who quit (Chaloupka, Cummings, Morley, & Horan, 2002; Fichtenberg & Glantz, 2002). With the experience of tobacco in mind, the field of prevention is looking for powerful policy and environmental strategies to prevent childhood obesity.

Understanding What Has Potential and Deserves Study. Whenever the prevention field lacks abundant evidence about effective policies, programs, or practices, we are often forced to refer repeatedly to the same promising examples. This is especially true in obesity prevention. The few community-based examples for which there is even a modest amount of evidence (such as Somerville, Massachusetts, and El Paso, Texas) have been cited frequently. This is not to discourage or minimize the impact these programs have had on the field, but the nation cannot and should not base its efforts on such limited experience. The Early Assessment initiative is the first step in identifying other possible examples because it identifies practice-based interventions that are worthy of additional evaluation.

People sometimes confuse evaluability assessments with full-scale evaluation (Shadish, Cook, & Leviton, 1991). This would be a serious misuse of the SSA Method, because "promise" does not mean the same thing as "effective." Evaluability assessments do not test outcomes, and they do not constitute an adequate test of implementation. Instead they assess the plausibility of a logic model, feasibility of implementation, and readiness for evaluation. Most important, the Early Assessment initiative found that numerous promising obesity prevention programs and policies could be identified in a short period of time and even prioritized for immediate and future comprehensive evaluation.

Identifying Unconventional Strategies. Until recently, research on obesity prevention focused primarily on didactic or experiential methods derived from behavioral theory. By contrast, the Early Assessment initiative concerned changes in children's environment that could enable a better diet and increase physical activity. Environmental changes rely on policies, a variety of financing instruments and approaches, city planning, and other fields of expertise that are far removed from conventional behavioral science. The initiative stimulated the expert panel to consider obesity prevention strategies outside of conventional behavioral science, and to expand the evaluation agenda for policy and environmental approaches. For example, the expert panel was particularly interested in the Food Trust's Pennsylvania Fresh Food Financing Initiative (FFFI), which to date has helped build more than 30 grocery stores in areas of Philadelphia that lack ready access to healthy food. FFFI's mission is to offer funding assistance and attract supermarket operators to underserved poor areas, thus improving both community economic development and access to healthy food. The reach of this initiative into vulnerable communities is significant, and the expert panel said it would be beneficial to learn what people purchase, if their purchasing patterns change, and the impact of the community economic development aspect of this program. Because the financing mechanism is sustainable and innovative, the expert panel suggested that the FFFI may be an opportunity for a prospective study as the initiative expands into other states, or for a pre-post time-series method looking at communities before, during, and after the store was established.

The expert panel was also particularly interested in the New York City Group Day Care Regulation (Amendments to Article 47 of the NYC Health Code). The innovative regulation mandates 60 minutes per day of physical activity, limited screen time, and reduced consumption of full-fat milk and sugar-sweetened beverages. The regulation has very high potential impact and significant reach because it is mandated and enforced in all licensed NYC group day care centers (currently more than 1,600), which include children from a range of races and socioeconomic levels. As a formal city regulation, the policy is permanent and therefore sustainable.

RWJF and CDC are currently funding ICF Macro to evaluate the day care regulation, to examine the extent of policy implementation and health outcomes for children. Evaluation planning and co-investigators include staff of the NYC Department of Health and Mental Hygiene's (NYC

DOHMH) Physical Activity and Nutrition Program, as well as a researcher who conducted a study of the regulations in 40 centers. The evaluation is a 3-year effort occurring in two phases. Phase 1 surveyed a stratified random sample of 200 of the approximately 1,650 registered day care centers in New York City. The project team collected data on engagement, capacity, technical assistance, and implementation via a review of each day care center's records, a site inventory, and surveys with center directors, food service staff, and teachers to determine "high" and "low" implementation. Additionally the team surveyed program staff and sanitarians who conduct the center inspections with the NYC DOHMH regarding training, technical assistance, and enforcement of the regulation. Phase 2 will be a longitudinal comparison of children's diet and physical activity in the high and low implementation centers. Twice per year for 2 years, the team will conduct child observations of diet, physical activity, and TV viewing screen time as well as measuring the children's height and weight. At 12 months (and possibly 24 months), the team also will survey center directors to confirm the level of implementation. This evaluation will yield empirical evidence regarding the health impact of the policy, will aid NYC DOHMH in determining any needed adjustments in enforcement and training practices, and will inform other jurisdictions that may consider instituting similar policies.

Neither the New York City Day Care regulations nor the FFFI relies on behavioral theory at its core. Yet both efforts have highly elaborated models that can plausibly affect large numbers of people. As described in Chapter 4, FFFI relied almost exclusively on advocacy, leveraging of financial resources, knowledge of the supermarket business, and the methods of economic development to create better access to food. In the same way, New York City's regulation of the day care environment and enforcement through inspection uses time-honored policies and practices of public health, not behavioral science—although to support implementation the city regularly trains day care staff on the SPARK preschool physical activity curriculum, which is partially based on behavioral research (Sallis et al., 1997; SPARK, 2004).

Reconsideration of Interventions. The initiative led to reconsideration of the potential for certain interventions to prevent childhood obesity. For example, a number of the expert panelists had previously dismissed farmers' markets as an ineffective strategy for obesity prevention. Yet they became intrigued with farmers' markets as a method to bring fresher, lower-calorie foods to inner-city areas that are underserved by supermarkets. There are limitations to how farmers' markets can change eating habits by themselves; they tend to occur once per week, they have limited offerings compared to supermarkets, the produce may be more expensive than that found in supermarkets, and in many areas of the country the season for such markets is far too short to promote true change in access to fresh food. However, farmers' markets, when implemented well, might introduce new foods and methods of preparation to populations that have been denied access to these foods in the past. As one outlet among many for food access (along with supermarkets, restaurants, and corner stores), farmers markets might work to change consumption patterns. If consumption patterns are the focus, then the issue becomes the relative impact of farmers' markets that are available year-round, as opposed to farmers' markets that are only available seasonally. Farmers' markets are not a single entity; they represent a class or type of intervention that may operate to prevent childhood obesity (see later discussion). Therefore, the expert panel recommended a cluster evaluation of various types of farmers' market programs to better determine what works to improve consumption of healthier foods and for whom. CDC is in the initial stages of evaluating farmers' markets to understand these issues better.

Understanding Common Challenges. The Early Assessment initiative revealed that even when some policies are established widely throughout policy sector, they are not necessarily well implemented. Such was the case for the school district local wellness policies, as mandated nationally by the Child Nutrition and Women, Infants, and Children Reauthorization Act of 2004 (Sec. 204 of P.L. 108–205). The law required that any school district participating in federally funded meal programs must establish a local wellness policy addressing physical activity opportunities outside of physical education, establishing nutrition guidelines for school meals, and limiting the high-calorie foods and beverages that "compete" with school meals. Although many school district local wellness policies were nominated as innovative and promising, closer examination indicated that those policies were difficult to implement and as a result relatively few were ready for evaluation. Other evidence confirms that nationally most local wellness policies still lack important components and have proven difficult to implement. Specifically, a nationally representative survey of 641 school districts in 2007–08 indicates that 95% of students were enrolled in a district with a wellness policy, but federally mandated components were lacking in a significant majority (Chriqui, Schneider, Chaloupka, Ide, & Pugach, 2009). In Arkansas and West Virginia, statewide evaluations of local school wellness policies have documented only gradual implementation (Raczynski et al., 2006, 2007, 2008; West Virginia University, 2009). Examination of comprehensive school physical activity programs also found limited implementation (National Association for Sport and Physical Education, 2008).

The Early Assessment initiative added value to our understanding of school health promotion strategy by permitting insight into barriers to, and facilitators of, implementation. Regarding barriers, although these policies have potential to improve physical activity level and food consumption practices in school districts across the United States, the reality is that without funding or accountability it is difficult to implement them and thus very few are viable evaluation investments. However, the facilitators are also important;

several school district local wellness policies and comprehensive school physical activity programs studied in the Early Assessment initiative cast light on what could be accomplished with adequate resources and commitment. Chapter 4 gave an example that merits evaluation; such evaluations are essential in guiding more effective school-based health promotion.

Impact on the Developers and Staff of Policy and Environmental Interventions

There were benefits for staff of the programs and policies that underwent evaluability assessments in the Early Assessment initiative. In a number of reports from the field, selection of the program by CDC for the initiative's site visit enhanced program visibility. The site visit summary report was sometimes used to justify future program operations. Program operators expressed appreciation that their interventions were highlighted in a CDC report shared with potential funders, and that their interventions were posted on a public health website as promising examples from the field (see the description below of North Carolina's Training and Research Translation Center).

The centerpiece of the SSA Method is evaluability assessment of the nominated programs and policies, to determine their readiness for evaluation and offer program-specific technical assistance. The evaluability assessment clarifies the goals and program design by specifying a program model, documenting stakeholders' views on the important issues, and exploring program reality (Leviton, Kettel Khan, Rog, Dawkins, & Cotton, in press; Patton, 1997; Wholey, 2004).

The 48 evaluability assessments of policy and environmental interventions helped focus attention on specific intervention components and operations that could be better aligned to meet the intervention's intended objectives. Through feedback and technical assistance, the Early Assessment initiative outlined what the intervention staff could do in the future to achieve that alignment. This is a program development activity, one that is a frequent consequence of evaluability assessments, and one that is underestimated in the evaluation literature (Leviton et al., in press; Smith, 1989). In general, project developers and managers appreciate these aspects of evaluability assessment (Leviton, Collins, Laird, & Kratt, 1998). In particular, we know that program staff value logic models (Carman & Fredericks, 2008), elicitation of which is an important product of evaluability assessments.

Feedback and technical assistance to the field was threaded throughout the initiative and was an opportunity to improve the quality and content of these programs and policies. The project's access to CDC technical assistance was a unique component of this initiative, modeled on experience in conducting evaluability assessments of nine worksite obesity prevention initiatives

(Hersey et al., 2008). To our knowledge, other evaluability assessments have not generally included technical assistance to developers and managers of the interventions, to expand on the feedback they receive. The site visit conversations, the evaluability assessment summary reports, and postvisit technical assistance teleconferences with CDC content experts generated real-time feedback and guidance that was well received and appreciated.

A survey of interventions studied in the first year of the initiative obtained 14 out of 23 responses, for a 61% response rate (ICF Macro, 2009). Several intervention staff reported that recognition by CDC and RWJF assisted them in getting resources and local credibility. Others valued documentation of their efforts, development of logic models, and suggestions for improvement based on the feedback and technical assistance that the initiative provided. All but one respondent rated both the logic model and the summary report as either somewhat useful or very useful. Of the 10 staff who rated the CDC technical assistance, all felt it was useful. Even if all the nonrespondents had a negative opinion of the initiative, these comments suggest that many of the staff valued the evaluability assessments.

Impact on the Field of Prevention Research

A Method to Acquire Practice-Based Evidence More Rapidly. As the nation grapples with identifying effective prevention strategies, there has been a call to augment our knowledge not solely with evidence-based practice but also with practice-based evidence. Practice-based evidence derives from real-world practices to complement highly controlled tests of behavioral theory. As noted in Chapter 1, the nation needs both approaches in developing strategies that are effective and realistic for broad implementation. The SSA Method assumes there is professional and practical wisdom about how to solve public health problems, and it can be tapped and systematized through the process of nomination, expert review, and documentation. Such procedures allow the field of prevention to gain knowledge more quickly and share this knowledge efficiently.

Recognition by Leading Prevention Researchers. A number of nationally recognized prevention research experts have been proponents of "translating practice into research" and have pointed to the Early Assessment initiative as an influential approach to increase the evidence base for obesity prevention (Glasgow et al., 2006). Lawrence W. Green, a long-time leader of the health promotion and disease prevention field, notes in a 2009 personal communication to the authors about his impressions of the project:

> Many community health interventions have had the luxury of building on a dutiful brick-by-brick accumulation of evidence from epidemiological studies and randomized trials of interventions. Occasionally an epidemic demands action in the relative absence of such evidence. Such was the case with HIV/AIDS in the 1980s; such might also have been the case with obesity at that

time had we recognized the growth of girth epidemic developing even then. Now that we have faced it as a public health crisis, we must also face the paucity of the kind of evidence-based practices that have become the gold standard of public health science and practice. We have no choice but to find other ways to educe evidence from the hundreds of innovative ideas sprouting in desperate communities across the country. Such was the challenge that CDC and the Robert Wood Johnson Foundation faced when they proposed to undertake an evaluability assessment of these innovations. As a former director of an office of CDC responsible for disseminating best practices in community and statewide tobacco control, I was convinced of the greater credibility and actionability of evaluation evidence from real-world communities in real-time programs with real public health workers, in contrast to highly controlled community trials with highly selected samples, highly trained and supervised staff and well subsidized operating budgets enriched with research funds. This evaluability assessment of existing programs has produced such a cadre of potentially powerful exemplars for the more rapid dissemination of practice-based evidence. If we want more evidence-based practices in obesity control, we will need such practice-based evidence. And at the rate the conventional method of building the brick-by-brick evidence from controlled trials is progressing, we will have no choice but to accept such practice-based evidence.

Green and other influential prevention researchers believe that the SSA Method is an important way to implement this principle. Ross Brownson, a leading researcher on policy and environmental approaches to prevention of chronic diseases, made this observation to the authors in 2009 when asked to comment on the value of the project:

The health consequences, prevalence, and trends in obesity are well-understood. What is much less known is what to do about this epidemic. Our repertoire of effective interventions to prevent obesity is quite limited. Therefore, a "bottom up" approach is needed to better describe and evaluate the effects of interventions that are occurring in real-world practice. This is where evaluability assessment becomes a crucial and timely tool. It allows us to categorize programs and policies according to their promise and readiness for evaluation. In particular, it gathers information often lacking on external validity, including factors such as: selection criteria and representativeness, staff characteristics, intervention content, costs, and program sustainability. The ability to advance the field of obesity prevention is greatly enhanced when we are able to more widely conduct evaluability assessments.

A pleasant surprise as the Early Assessment initiative progressed was that a number of prevention researchers recognized these challenges and the potential for the SSA Method to help address them. The initiative benefited greatly from the participation of senior public health researchers and practitioners, both in the expert panels and in conducting evaluability assessments.

These participants brought an array of expertise and experience to a process that highlighted their knowledge about what was truly feasible in the field. National experts who advised the project said they better understood real-world practice and expanded their awareness of its potential, as they discussed nominations, shared experiences from the field, and came to final conclusions about which interventions could plausibly contribute to childhood obesity prevention. The experts who have worked with the project found they benefited from the process because it stimulated discussion of what is viable evidence, what outcomes are appropriate, and what expectations should be when public health professionals and researchers work to develop and assist community programs.

Impact on CDC's Chronic Disease Activities. The staff of the CDC National Center for Chronic Disease Prevention and Health Promotion who worked on the project found evaluability assessment a useful addition to the evaluation repertoire. Conducting evaluability assessments gave them a concrete overview of the potential uses of this method and has created a cadre of public health professionals from a variety of backgrounds who are familiar with the method. In addition, staff members of the CDC Division of Heart Disease and Stroke Prevention are implementing the SSA Method to identify emerging evidence in the field in cardiovascular disease prevention.

CDC staff has become familiar with a range of new policy and environmental interventions in prevention. The Division of Nutrition, Physical Activity, and Obesity is now supporting evaluation of three of these projects, with plans for more. Further, the CDC Prevention Research Centers (PRC) have indicated they would like to explore partnering with some of the policies and programs that were deemed promising to further develop and position them for more rigorous study. In particular, the University of North Carolina's Center for Excellence in Training and Research Translation (TRT), led by Alice Ammerman, will describe as many of these programs and policies on its website as funding permits (six are currently being developed), identifying them as promising interventions that warrant evaluation. The website includes a practice review tool so that others in the field can learn about the strategies and operations of these promising programs and policies (www.center-trt.org).

Implications of the SSA Method for Evaluation Practice

The Early Assessment initiative taught the developers of SSA about the extent to which the method could achieve its aspirations and about important considerations in making it operational. Adaptations of the method are under way for cardiovascular disease prevention, nursing education, and prevention of intimate partner violence in immigrant populations. However, none of these efforts is likely to have the scope of the Early Assessment initiative, and adaptations will require abbreviation or elimination of some steps in the process. Therefore, the initiative offers the most complete example to assess the place of the SSA Method in evaluation practice.

NEW DIRECTIONS FOR EVALUATION • DOI: 10.1002/ev

Reducing Uncertainty About Where to Focus Evaluation. Utility is the primary justification for evaluations. Yet all too often, the utility of evaluations is confined to single uses of single studies. To develop more definitive information about these innovations to encourage their dissemination and spread, we need portfolios that include evaluation of many interventions. The SSA Method aims to provide such a portfolio. Cronbach (1982) recommended that priority for evaluation resources should be assigned on the basis of prior information about the most important areas to increase knowledge and on the prior probability that the evaluations will be concretely useful. We conclude that the SSA Method as applied to childhood obesity prevention was successful in this regard. More generally, uncertainty reduction appears to be a good practice to find programs and policies worth evaluating. The initiative improved the prior probability of evaluating effective interventions by gathering information about the plausibility of effects (given the logic model, resources, and activities), likely generalizability, feasibility of implementation, and other criteria described in Chapters 1 and 2. The method also reduced uncertainty in a different way, by highlighting some of the most important information needs and gaps in understanding for a new field of inquiry.

Challenging Expert Assumptions. Central to the uniqueness of the Systematic Screening and Assessment Method is use of an expert panel to review and select potential programs and policies. An unexpected outcome of this review process was that the experts shifted or reframed their assumptions, expectations, and knowledge of the field. They were stimulated to consider interventions differently than they had done prior to the panel discussions. We believe this is likely to happen as the SSA Method is applied to other areas, as well. We have described the expert panel debate about farmers' markets; real-world examples and how-to information helped to revise expectations about this intervention type. The nominations and evaluability assessments of school district local wellness policies also challenged the expert panel's assumptions; both the Early Assessment staff and the expert panel initially believed these policies were a strong and viable mechanism to improve nutrition and physical activity through the public schools. The project received an extraordinary number of nominations ($n = 146$), which should have been indicative of a great number of school districts offering healthy food and physical activity environments for children. However, when critically reviewed, these nominations lacked innovation, depth, and strong implementation, resulting in only six candidates to undergo evaluability assessment. In particular, many of the submitted policies did not fully meet the policy requirements. Of the six visited, four were deemed ready for evaluation.

Evaluations are most often useful for conceptual purposes related to potential for program impact, for stakeholders to seriously consider information, or to change decision-maker assumptions (Shadish et al., 1991). However, formal evaluations are substantially more costly than evaluability assessments, which seem to have served this purpose in certain cases in the Early Assessment initiative.

Developing Research and Evaluation Agendas for Policy and Practice. The SSA Method aspires to create research agendas by stimulating discussion of research questions about interventions and design strategies for evaluation. We conclude that the initiative was successful in fulfilling this aspiration. The expert panel discussions went far beyond review of the individual programs and policies that were nominated. These experts are in the business of knowledge development, which implies close attention to theory, causal relationships, and generalizability. Yet they were fascinated by practice, which enlarged their views about the most powerful policies and programs that might work to reverse the obesity epidemic. For example, the expert panelists were especially interested in exploring programs that were particularly innovative, that involved unique partnerships or coalitions, or that relied on a variety of financing instruments for growth and spread. Although not all such programs were selected for an evaluability assessment, there was genuine interest in learning more about how these programs were started and operated and their potential to influence future research questions.

The research agenda that emerged included questions about individual interventions, and about types or classes of interventions. As the nomination and screening process unfolded, it quickly became apparent that the interventions fell into several classes or types. These types can be differentiated by their sharing an underlying logic model or theory of change, with some variation among exemplars of a type. Chapter 3 includes some examples of generic logic models for such intervention types. In a single content area, there could be several such types. For example, the content area "food access" includes at least three types: farmers' markets, restaurant programs, and supermarket programs. All three types share the goal of increasing the availability of healthy foods in lower-income communities, but each type has a distinct logic model (with variation across exemplars of the type). The content area "child care settings" includes two intervention types: after-school programs and day care programs and policies. "School-based health promotion" as studied in the Early Assessment initiative includes two types: school district local wellness policies and comprehensive school physical activity curricula.

The expert panel created research agendas for understanding several common intervention types. For example, the panel suggested that a typology of logic models may be useful for the after-school and day care programs. They suggested comparing after-school programs that use parks and recreation facilities to those confined to the school setting only. The facilities, staff, and competing priorities might be very different; for example, tutoring and homework might dominate the school-based programs, with physical activity as an afterthought. Additionally, programs might focus on nutrition rather than physical activity, or on both.

NEW DIRECTIONS FOR EVALUATION • DOI: 10.1002/ev

The expert panelists also suggested studying the logic models for each of the three intervention types dealing with access to healthier food: farmers' markets, restaurant programs, and supermarket programs. The research questions about farmers' markets have already been described, but in addition the panel discussed the potential of evaluating all of the food access programs together for their advantages and disadvantages. Furthermore, the panel members wondered: What is the impact and process utility of food access programs that feature electronic benefits transfer (EBT) cards, which make it easier for federal food program recipients to purchase food? EBT machines were being introduced to farmers' markets, but there were challenges. The expert panel wanted to know whether programs that featured EBT could allow cost recovery by having the EBT machine use be optional for all paying customers, like a credit card. They wanted to understand the programs that featured various financing techniques to build facilities and start food outlets. How do these financing techniques work? How do such programs get started? How can the variety of lending and financing instruments be used more generally to promote development of supermarkets in low-income areas, or contribute to the spread of other food access interventions?

This discussion also led to questions about the science around the relationship between increased access to fruits and vegetables and childhood obesity. Specifically, the expert panelists wondered: Is an increase in access to fruits and vegetables sufficient to improve their consumption, and does greater consumption of fruits and vegetables prevent obesity? What is known is that populations with greater access to foods, in particular supermarkets, purchase greater amounts of fruits and vegetables (Morland, Wing, & Diez-Roux, 2002). People who eat more fruits and vegetables are less likely to be obese (Ledikwe et al., 2006). Also, a diet that is based on decreased energy density achieved primarily by increased consumption of fruits and vegetables leads to weight loss (Ello-Martin, Roe, Ledikwe, Beach, & Rolls, 2007).

Conclusion

In prevention research and evaluation, choices must always be made about what to evaluate, given the available limited resources. The ultimate result of the Systematic Screening and Assessment Method is to create better conditions for useful evaluations of strong, promising practices. In a time of budget constraints and competition for limited resources, a process that increases the likelihood of identifying successful programs and policies for evaluation is valuable. Also, time is of the essence in our drive to build the evidence base for viable, feasible, reliable, and specific community-based obesity prevention strategies. We need to know what is required to answer these important questions, and we need to know what method may be most appropriate relative to the program realities we have witnessed and analyzed. The SSA Method aimed to achieve these goals more quickly, more effectively, and more strategically.

References

Carman, J. G., & Fredericks, K. A. (2008). Nonprofits and evaluation: Empirical evidence from the field, In J. G. Carman & K. A. Fredericks (ed.), *Nonprofits and evaluation. New Directions for Evaluation, 119*, 51–72.

Chaloupka, F. J., Cummings, K. M., Morley, C. P., & Horan, J. K. (2002). Tax, price and cigarette smoking: Evidence from the tobacco documents and implications for tobacco company marketing strategies. *British Medical Journal, 11*(Supplement 1), i62–i72.

Cheung, K., Dawkins, N., Kettel Khan, L., & Leviton, L. (2009). *Early Assessment of Programs and Policies to Prevent Childhood Obesity Evaluability Assessment Synthesis Report: Increasing access to healthy foods*. Atlanta: U.S. Department of Health and Human Services, Centers for Disease Control and Prevention.

Chriqui, J. F., Schneider, L., Chaloupka, F. J., Ide, K., & Pugach, O. (2009). *Local wellness policies: Assessing school district strategies for improving children's health. School years 2006–07 and 2007–08*. Chicago: Bridging the Gap, Health Policy Center, Institute for Health Research and Policy.

Cronbach, L. J. (1982). *Designing evaluations of educational and social programs*. San Francisco: Jossey-Bass.

Ello-Martin, J. A., Roe, L. S., Ledikwe, J. H., Beach, A. M., & Rolls, B. (2007). Dietary energy density in the treatment of obesity: A year-long trial comparing 2 weight-loss diets. *American Journal of Clinical Nutrition, 85*, 1465–1477.

Fichtenberg, C. M., & Glantz, S. A. (2002). Effect of smoke-free workplaces on smoking behavior: Systematic review. *British Medical Journal, 325*, 188–191.

Glasgow, R. E., Green, L. W., Klesges, L. W., Abrams, D. B., Fisher, E. B., Goldstein, M. B., et al. (2006). External validity: We need to do more. *Annals of Behavioral Medicine, 3*, 12.

Glasgow, R. E., Vogt, T. M., & Boles, S. M. (1999). Evaluating the public health impact of health promotion interventions: The RE-AIM framework. *American Journal of Public Health, 89*, 1323–1327.

Hersey, J., Williams-Peihota, P., Sparling P. B., Alexander, J., Hill, M. D., Isenberg, K. B., et al. (2008). Promising practices in promotion of healthy weight at small and medium-sized U.S. worksites. *Prevention of Chronic Disease, 5*(4), A122.

ICF Macro. (2009). *Assessing the influences of evaluability assessment: An exploratory study of changes in organizational attitudes and behaviors towards program evaluation*. Atlanta: Author.

Koplan, J. P., Liverman, C. T., & Kraak, V. I. (2005). *Preventing childhood obesity: Health in the balance*. Washington, DC: National Academies Press.

Ledikwe, J. H., Blanck, H. M., Kettel Khan, L., Serdula, M. K., Seymour, J. D., Tohill, B. C., et al. (2006). Dietary energy density is associated with energy intake and weight status in U.S. adults. *American Journal of Clinical Nutrition, 83*, 1362–1368.

Leviton, L. C., Collins, C., Laird, B., & Kratt, P. (1998). Teaching evaluation using evaluability assessment. *Evaluation, 4*(4), 389–409.

Leviton, L. C., Kettel Khan, L., Rog, D., Dawkins, N., & Cotton, D. (in press). Evaluability assessment to improve public health. *Annual Review of Public Health, 31*.

Morland, K., Wing, S., & Diez-Roux, A. (2002). The contextual effect of the local food environment on residents' diets: The Atherosclerosis Risk in Communities Study. *American Journal of Public Health, 92*(11), 1761–1767.

National Association for Sport and Physical Education. (2008). *Comprehensive School Physical Activity Programs* [position statement]. Reston, VA: Author.

Patton, M. Q. (1997). *Utilization-focused evaluation: The new century text*. Thousand Oaks, CA: Sage.

Pitt Barnes, S., Robin, L., Dawkins, N., Leviton, L., & Kettel Khan, L. (2009a). *Early Assessment of Programs and Policies to Prevent Childhood Obesity Evaluability Assessment*

Synthesis Report: Comprehensive physical activity programs. Atlanta: U.S. Department of Health and Human Services, Centers for Disease Control and Prevention.

Pitt Barnes, S., Robin, L., Dawkins, N., Leviton, L., & Kettel Khan, L. (2009b). *Early Assessment of Programs and Policies to Prevent Childhood Obesity Evaluability Assessment Synthesis Report: Local wellness policy.* Atlanta: U.S. Department of Health and Human Services, Centers for Disease Control and Prevention.

Raczynski, J. M., Phillips, M., Bursac, Z., Kahn, R. A., Pulley, L., West, D., et al. (2006). *Year three evaluation: Arkansas Act 1220 of 2003 to Combat Childhood Obesity.* Little Rock: University of Arkansas for Medical Sciences. Retrieved June 30, 2009, from http://www.uams.edu/coph/reports/2006Act1220_Year3.pdf

Raczynski, J. M., Phillips, M., Bursac, Z., Kahn, R. A., Pulley, L., West, D., et al. (2007). *Year four evaluation: Arkansas Act 1220 of 2003 to Combat Childhood Obesity.* Little Rock: University of Arkansas for Medical Sciences. Retrieved June 30, 2009, from http://www.uams.edu/coph/reports/Act1220/COPH%202007%20Obesity%20Evalua tion%20Report.pdf

Raczynski, J. M., Phillips, M., Bursac, Z., Kahn, R. A., Pulley, L., West, D., et al. (2008). *Year five evaluation: Arkansas Act 1220 of 2003 to Combat Childhood Obesity.* Little Rock: University of Arkansas for Medical Sciences. Retrieved June 30, 2009, from http://www.uams.edu/coph/reports/ACT%201220%20Year%205%20executive%20sum mary.pdf

Sallis, J. F., McKenzie, T. L., Alcaraz, J. E., Kolody, B., Faucette, N., & Hovell, M. F. (1997). The effects of a 2-year physical education program (SPARK) on physical activity and fitness in elementary school students. *American Journal of Public Health, 87,* 1328–1334.

Shadish, W. R., Cook, T. D., & Leviton, L. C. (1991). *Foundations of program evaluation: Theorists and their theories.* Thousand Oaks, CA: Sage.

Skelton, S., Dawkins, N., Leviton, L., & Kettel Khan, L. (2009). *Early Assessment of Programs and Policies to Prevent Childhood Obesity Evaluability Assessment Synthesis Brief: Built environment and land use.* Atlanta: U.S. Department of Health and Human Services, Centers for Disease Control and Prevention.

Smith, M. F. (1989). *Evaluability assessment: A practical approach.* Boston: Kluwer Academic.

SPARK. (2004). The SPARK Early Childhood Physical Activity Program. Retrieved June 1, 2009, from www.sparkpe.org/programEarlyChildhood.jsp

West Virginia University, Robert C. Byrd Health Sciences Center. (2009). Evaluation of West Virginia Lifestyles Act of 2005: Executive summary. Morgantown, WV: Author. Retrieved June 30, 2009, from www.rwjf.org/files/research/386733727wva healthylifestylesyr1exsum.pdf

Wethington, H., Hall, M., Dawkins, N., Leviton, L., & Kettel Khan, L. (2009). *Early Assessment of Programs and Policies to Prevent Childhood Obesity Evaluability Assessment Synthesis Report: Childcare initiatives in afterschool and daycare settings.* Atlanta: U.S. Department of Health and Human Services, Centers for Disease Control and Prevention.

Wholey, J. S. (2004) Evaluability assessment. In J. S. Wholey, H. P. Hatry, & K. E. Newcomer, *Handbook of practical program evaluation* (pp. 33–62). San Francisco: Jossey-Bass.

LAURA KETTEL KHAN *is currently the Senior Scientist for Policy and Partnerships in the Division of Nutrition, Physical Activity, and Obesity at the Centers
for Disease Control and Prevention (CDC), the primary public health agency
working to prevent obesity and chronic diseases in the United States.*

NICOLA DAWKINS *is a Principal of ICF Macro, where she designs and implements
research and evaluation studies and led Macro's team in coordinating the Robert
Wood Johnson Foundation/CDC initiative Early Assessment of Programs and
Policies to Prevent Childhood Obesity.*

LAURA C. LEVITON *is the coauthor of* Foundations of Program Evaluation *and
is currently Special Advisor for Evaluation at the Robert Wood Johnson Foundation where for the past 10 years she has overseen more than 80 evaluations
at national, state, and local levels.*

NEW DIRECTIONS FOR EVALUATION • DOI: 10.1002/ev

Rog, D. J. (2010). The SSA Method: Not just old wine in a new bottle. In L. C. Leviton, L. Kettel Khan, & N. Dawkins (Eds.), *The Systematic Screening and Assessment Method: Finding innovations worth evaluating. New Directions for Evaluation, 125*, 111–118.

6

The SSA Method: Not Just Old Wine in a New Bottle

Debra J. Rog

Abstract

The Systematic Screening and Assessment (SSA) Method is a novel application of evaluability assessment (EA), entwined with the work of an expert panel that nominates programs worthy of EA and then, on the basis of the findings from the EAs, recommends programs for evaluation. The author compares and contrasts the SSA Method with the usual practice of EA and discusses how the method has contributed to the revival of EA in recent years. © Wiley Periodicals, Inc., and the American Evaluation Association

At the heart of the Systematic Screening and Assessment (SSA) Method is evaluability assessment (EA), intertwined with the work of an expert panel that nominates programs worthy of EA and then, on the basis of the findings from the EAs, recommends programs for evaluation. As a long-time proponent of the use of EA (Rog, 1985) and one that has watched its ebb and flow over the past three decades (Rog, 2005), I am encouraged by this reworking of the method. In addition, as a panelist on an expert panel, I was afforded the opportunity to witness this method in action, and in particular observe the function of the expert panel.

In this chapter, I first place the SSA Method within the context of the history of EA and distinguish its use from the conventional role of EA. I then describe the situations that appear most appropriate for the SSA Method and highlight the method's adaptations of EA that are noteworthy. Also noted are elements of EA that do not appear to be central to the SSA Method but have value in other EA situations. Finally, I recognize the value of the SSA Method in re-invigorating EA and outline the variety of roles EA can play in current domestic and international evaluation arenas.

The SSA Method Within the Context of EA's History and Use

Evaluability assessment (EA), developed by Joseph Wholey and colleagues (e.g., Wholey, 2004), was used extensively in the mid-1970s and early 1980s in the federal government, especially by the Department of Health and Human Services (Rog, 1985). It was also used widely by the Canadian government.

EA was developed in response to the lack of use of findings from evaluation studies. Exploring this issue, Wholey and colleagues found that a large number of evaluation studies yielded null or negative results. Among the reasons were evaluations of programs that were not fully implemented or did not even exist, evaluations based on the "grant goals" of a program that were far-flung and unrealistic, and evaluations of programs that lacked a basic underlying logic. In addition, the exploration revealed that there was inadequate ownership of the evaluation findings on the part of key stakeholders, which was in part due to little agreement in the outcomes examined.

The key tenets of the EA method as originally designed are to:

- Document program design
- Document the program as implemented
- Examine the measurement and information systems
- Analyze the plausibility that the program as implemented can achieve the goals (given prior research and theory, common sense, context, timeframe, and resources available)
- Develop options for strengthening program theory, improving program implementation, building evaluation capacity, and conducting evaluation

EA was designed to assess the logic of an intervention and its plausibility in achieving the goals for which it is designed. It is a key method for determining the extent to which a program is ready for an evaluation (typically an outcome evaluation), the changes that are needed to increase its readiness, and the type of evaluation approach most suitable to judge performance of a program or policy.

Although the method was used less frequently in the late 1980s and 1990s, it appears to be reemerging in both public and private sectors as a method for learning about an intervention quickly and how best to evaluate it (Leviton, Kettel Khan, Rog, Dawkins, & Cotton, in press; Rog, 2005). Some of the recent impetus for EA at the federal level appears to be the Program Assessment Rating Tool (PART) and the Government Performance Results Act (GPRA). Both initiatives place emphasis on evaluation of all programs and policies, even programs that may have been in existence for 20 years, such as the Community Mental Health Block Grant Program (Mulkern, 2005). In some of these situations, EA has been rediscovered as a tool to guide planning of evaluation. As a systematic method for assessing a program's reality, EA has been found especially useful in situations where implementation of a program has likely shifted over time from initial design and legislative goals.

The SSA Method is a special application in this revival of EA. In conventional EA, the purpose is to review the logic and implementation of a program (or sometimes of a project within a program) to assess whether it is ready for an evaluation or to plan for subsequent evaluation. Evaluations are commissioned for many purposes, among them determination of accountability, program improvement, and learning about an intervention. In the case of the SSA Method as described in this issue, however, the focus of subsequent evaluations is almost squarely on knowledge production for a field of practice. In addition, whereas EA can be used in a range of evaluation situations—both single program and multisite programs—the method is most appropriate for use by funders who are interested in scanning the field for programs that are developed from the ground up. Moreover, it is most appropriate for intervention areas where little is known about effectiveness, or about the mechanisms for achieving effectiveness.

The SSA Method: Methodological Adaptations to EA

Much of the process of the SSA Method reflects the basic tenets of EA as described above. There are a few key adaptations and elaborations in the issue, however, that are particularly noteworthy.

Melding EA With the Use of an Expert Panel. In conventional EA, there is an emphasis on engaging a program's stakeholders in the process. Wholey (1979) emphasized the use of a work group to engage those stakeholders closest to the program in the EA process, and a policy group to inform higher-level policy makers of what is being learned through the EA. Because the SSA Method is applied to an area of intervention rather than a specific program, including program stakeholders in the process is less relevant. The most appropriate stakeholders for the SSA Method are individuals with expertise in the types of interventions with promise in an area and with an understanding of how best to affect an issue.

Having Programs Nominated and Then Reviewed for EA Inclusion. In the SSA Method, programs are first nominated for their promise by outside individuals and then screened by an expert panel according to many of the criteria that will be examined in depth in the EA. The fact that programs are screened for their "EA worthiness" likely translates into programs that have a much greater possibility of being "evaluable" than examining a broader swath of existing programs without prior review.

Providing Details on Training and Implementation. Chapters 3 and 4 in this issue present extremely helpful specifics on training and implementation that are often learned only after implementing one or more EAs. These chapters offer the reader a fly-on-the-wall perspective from the experiences of this research team. Chapter 3 lays out helpful details on the training and preparation activities that need to take place, when they must occur, and who is responsible for making them happen. In addition, Table 3.4, with its outline of the summary report, gives readers a practical tool for approaching summaries of any EA, not just the SSA Method.

Chapter 3 is not only useful in delineating the steps to the process that was used to train EA site visitors, but also in highlighting those areas that need particular attention, such as refresher sessions when multiple EAs are conducted, and additional training on qualitative interviewing and development of logic models. The latter area is especially important; many evaluators conducting EAs may be tempted to skirt basic training in interviewing and logic models if the trainees are individuals seasoned in evaluation. The experience of the authors suggests, however, that those with education and experience in program evaluation do not always have the requisite experience with these methods. This tip is important for EA training overall, not just the SSA Method, and suggests that inclusion of basic review topics is critical to any training. Finally, the examples of use of EA in the field that are found in Chapter 4 offer tips for evaluators in implementing EA. For example, the authors describe several different approaches to collaboratively developing a logic model with stakeholders and the flexibility needed by the evaluation team. For the Pennsylvania Food Financing Initiative, for example, the draft model developed by the EA team underwent extensive revisions as the EA team together with the program staff carefully reviewed the model. One area of expansion, for example, involved dividing the inputs into those needed to get funding from the legislature for the program, and then those needed to implement the program. The joint group then made sure that each input was then associated with an activity or process, outputs and outcomes. In the second example of the NYC Day Care Regulations, however, the logic model discussion was brief and only minor suggestions were offered. In yet the third example, the key stakeholders agreed with the goals outlined in the model (in part because the policy materials clearly articulated them) but had many concerns about detailing specific outcomes in the absence of baseline data. Thus, general outcomes were put on the model as place holders until more specific, evaluable ones could be developed.

Distinguishing Plausibility and Feasibility. SSA employs a helpful distinction between plausibility and feasibility, and how the method assesses both of these concepts. Plausibility refers to whether a program is expected to achieve the outcomes it intends to achieve, and feasibility refers to whether the program can be implemented as intended. These concepts are often confused, and clarification is important. It is also important to note, however, that feasibility could also refer to whether a subsequent evaluation is feasible—that is, even if an EA finds that the plausibility of a program achieving its intended outcomes is good, it may still not be a candidate for evaluation because the conditions may not be in place to support rigorous evaluation. The term *evaluation capacity* describes the concept of evaluation feasibility.

Synthesis of the EAs. EA is not an evaluation; it does not conduct an assessment of a program's worth or effectiveness. An EA, however, can yield useful information about an intervention: how it is designed, whether it can be implemented as designed, and the plausibility of its achieving outcomes. When a number of EAs are conducted within a field of practice, as in the case of the SSA Method, looking across the results of these efforts can establish valuable information on the state of practice within the field. This is particularly the case in areas where little evaluation has taken place and the action in programming has sprung from the field. Conducting a number of EAs and a subsequent synthesis can help to generate information for policy makers, funders, and program developers on what interventions are in place and appear to be most promising as they await data on those interventions that are most effective.

EA Elements Revisited

Analysis of Plausibility. For most of the EAs in the SSA Method, plausibility could be established and thus the three examples illustrate promising and potentially effective approaches. It is likely that the nomination process and the expert panel prescreening produced greater guarantees that the programs going through the EA process will be plausible and promising interventions.

In other EA situations, however, the linkage between the program activities and outcomes is likely more tenuous. It is helpful for readers to have an understanding of what poor plausibility looks like and to expect "chinks in the links" between activities and outcomes. For example, in a set of pilot EAs in childhood obesity prevention conducted to guide the SSA Method, a number of the programs reviewed had issues with plausibility. Some programs suffered from incomplete logic in their design—for example, some community garden programs had childhood obesity prevention as a goal but had no explicit activities for children to eat the food or engage in greater physical activity than they would do if they were not involved in the gardens. Other programs had plausibility issues due to a lack of follow-through in the activities—for example, some school programs training teachers to incorporate physical activity in their class curriculum but not incorporating any organizational supports that allow teachers to implement the programs.

In assessing plausibility, it is important to develop a logic model that displays the program as the program developers view it and as it is implemented. There is often a tendency for evaluators to want to fill in the logic and make assumptions that may not in fact be in operation. In EA, it is important to leave gaps alone, even if this may be awkward or embarrassing for the program. Not all programs are developed with a clear, logical design, and outcomes may remain in a program's rhetoric without explicit attachment to activities, along with activities having no clear logical linkage to outcomes. In addition, changes in program funding over time can weaken certain activities to the point that achievement of intended outcomes is questionable, but no changes have been made to the stated outcomes. The point is that an evaluator conducting an EA must develop a model that displays a program as it is and not force a logic.

Intended Uses of Evaluation. Another aspect of the EA methodology that is not as relevant to the SSA Method but is important in other EA situations is the relationship of use to evaluability. In SSA, the intent is to identify programs that can promote the best evaluation situation and add to our understanding of an area of intervention. In most EAs, the purpose is to determine if a particular program is ready for evaluation. Part of the readiness assessment is to determine whether there are users for the evaluation information. Are there stakeholders who can use the information and either improve the program or act on the outcome findings? If it is not likely that action will take place according to the findings of an evaluation, it may not be worth conducting the program even if it seems well suited to achieve an outcome.

Recommended Options. In conventional EAs, there is an emphasis on recommending what is needed to make a program evaluable if it is not fully ready for an evaluation. These are often referred to as "options" for the program to consider. They include program design options to strengthen or modify the design and goals of a program or policy to align with desired outcomes; program management options to improve implementation or management of a program or policy; and measurement options to develop and enhance data systems. In the SSA Method, it appears as though options were part of the technical assistance built into the process, especially for those programs that would not be nominated for evaluation. In most EAs, these options are relevant even when a program may be evaluable and recommended for evaluation.

Spurring New Uses for EA

EA is conventionally regarded as a method for determining whether a program is ready for an outcome evaluation and for planning that evaluation. The SSA Method sheds light on another use for a modified EA approach, namely identifying prospects in a field of intervention that might offer the best cases for rigorous evaluation and learning.

Over the years, those working with EA have found that it can be a useful tool, either in its entirety or with adaptation for a range of other evaluation situations. For example, in developing a program the developer can incorporate explicit attention to how best to enhance the program's plausibility of achieving outcomes. This takes understanding of the existing evidence base in the program area as well as understanding of the context within which a program is being implemented, including the resources and time available. It also means incorporating into the program systematic data collection that may aid both formative and summative evaluation. In addition, as a program is implemented, having an EA perspective means that any changes in program operations from what was initially designed should spark attention to determine whether changes should also be made in the expected outputs, as well as short-term and long-term outcomes.

In my own work, we adapted the SSA Method to identify medical respite care programs for homeless individuals that could be studied retrospectively. As in the case of obesity prevention, medical respite care is an intervention that has emerged from the ground up on the part of providers who saw the need for recuperative care for individuals discharged from the hospital to the street or a shelter. A variety of medical respite care approaches have been developed and a network of providers has emerged in the National Healthcare for the Homeless Council. Very little research in this area has been conducted. A notable exception is a study of a medical respite care program in Chicago that yielded positive results, spurring the U.S. Department of Health and Human Services to fund an effort to identify and study three to five additional programs. An expert panel worked with us to develop the criteria for selecting programs that met some basic standards of medical respite care. To identify programs that met these criteria, as well as criteria of readiness for the type of retrospective evaluation we were slated to conduct, we engaged in what we referred to as "EA lite" studies. They involved conducting document reviews and extensive telephone interviews with key staff in a candidate program. From these studies, we identified several candidates and began data collection. Therefore, in multisite studies EA can be used as a first step in determining which sites should be included. This is similar to the SSA application, although for some multisite program situations the focus is likely to be on the program sites *not* to include in the evaluation, rather than selecting one or two of the best cases to include.

Yet another use for EA is as proof of concept. Moran (2005) and colleagues, for example, used EA as a way to investigate whether discharge planning as a process could (1) be identified and measured across a range of settings and (2) be plausibly linked to prevention of homelessness. In this type of application, the interest is in determining whether the concept is indeed one that can be measured, if it makes sense, and if it would be feasible to study.

NEW DIRECTIONS FOR EVALUATION • DOI: 10.1002/ev

Summary

SSA contributes significantly to the literature on EA. It offers a method for approaching a new field of intervention and contributing to the knowledge base systematically and cost-effectively. The detail on training and implementation within SSA gives up-to-date guidance in how to use EA, not only within the SSA framework but for most applications of the core method.

Probably most important, SSA revitalizes EA. EA is a tool that evaluators and funders are rediscovering, to use for its original purpose as an evaluation planning tool as well as in adaptations that fit different program and policy situations. In all of its uses, EA generally is a method that helps guide more intelligent use of resources, is flexible in how it can be implemented, provides both written and visual products that can communicate findings succinctly and directly, and incorporates stakeholders in a meaningful and important way.

References

Leviton, L. C., Kettel Khan, L., Rog, D., Dawkins, N., & Cotton, D. (in press). Evaluability assessment to improve public health. *Annual Review of Public Health, 31*.

Moran, G. (2005, October). *Assessing the effectiveness of discharge planning to prevent homelessness: An evaluability assessment*. Presented at the Joint Meeting of the Canadian Evaluation Society and the American Evaluation Association, Toronto.

Mulkern, V. (2005, October). *Evaluability assessment of the Community Mental Health Block Grant Program*. Presented at the Joint Meeting of the Canadian Evaluation Society and the American Evaluation Association, Toronto.

Rog, D. J. (1985). *A methodological analysis of evaluability assessment*. Unpublished Ph.D. thesis, Vanderbilt University.

Rog, D. J. (2005, October). *Evaluability assessment: Then and now*. Presented at the Joint Meeting of the Canadian Evaluation Society and the American Evaluation Association, Toronto.

Wholey, J. S. (1979). *Evaluation: Promise and performance*. Washington, DC: Urban Institute.

Wholey, J. S. (2004). Assessing the feasibility and likely usefulness of evaluation. In J. S. Wholey, H. P. Hatry, & K. E. Newcomer (Eds.), *Handbook of practical program evaluation*. San Francisco: Jossey-Bass.

DEBRA J. ROG *is the 2009 President of the American Evaluation Association and Vice President of the Rockville Institute for the Advancement of Social Science, a nonprofit corporation affiliated with Westat.*

INDEX

ORDER FORM SUBSCRIPTION AND SINGLE ISSUES

DISCOUNTED BACK ISSUES:

Use this form to receive 20% off all back issues of *New Directions for Evaluation*.
All single issues priced at **$23.20** (normally $29.00)

TITLE	ISSUE NO.	ISBN
_____	_____	_____
_____	_____	_____
_____	_____	_____

Call 888-378-2537 or see mailing instructions below. When calling, mention the promotional code JBXND to receive your discount. For a complete list of issues, please visit www.josseybass.com/go/ndev

SUBSCRIPTIONS: (1 YEAR, 4 ISSUES)

☐ New Order ☐ Renewal

U.S.	☐ Individual: $85	☐ Institutional: $256
CANADA/MEXICO	☐ Individual: $85	☐ Institutional: $296
ALL OTHERS	☐ Individual: $109	☐ Institutional: $330

*Call 888-378-2537 or see mailing and pricing instructions below.
Online subscriptions are available at www.interscience.wiley.com*

ORDER TOTALS:

Issue / Subscription Amount: $ _____

Shipping Amount: $ _____
(for single issues only — subscription prices include shipping)

Total Amount: $ _____

SHIPPING CHARGES:

	SURFACE	DOMESTIC	CANADIAN
First Item		$3.00	$6.00
Each Add'l Item		$3.00	$1.50

(No sales tax for U.S. subscriptions. Canadian residents, add GST for subscription orders. Individual rate subscriptions must be paid by personal check or credit card. Individual rate subscriptions may not be resold as library copies.)

BILLING & SHIPPING INFORMATION:

☐ **PAYMENT ENCLOSED:** *(U.S. check or money order only. All payments must be in U.S. dollars.)*

☐ **CREDIT CARD:** ☐ VISA ☐ MC ☐ AMEX

Card number _____ Exp. Date _____

Card Holder Name _____ Card Issue # *(required)* _____

Signature _____ Day Phone _____

☐ **BILL ME:** *(U.S. institutional orders only. Purchase order required.)*

Purchase order # _____
Federal Tax ID 13559302 • GST 89102-8052

Name _____

Address _____

Phone _____ E-mail _____

Copy or detach page and send to: **John Wiley & Sons, PTSC, 5th Floor**
989 Market Street, San Francisco, CA 94103-1741

Order Form can also be faxed to: **888-481-2665**

PROMO JBXND

JB JOSSEY-BASS™

▸ New and Noteworthy Titles in **Research Methods**

Research Essentials: An Introduction to Designs and Practices,
Stephen D. Lapan (Editor), MaryLynn T. Quartaroli (Editor), ISBN: 9780470181096, Paperback, 384 pages, 2009, $75.00.

Research Methods for Everyday Life: Blending Qualitative and Quantitative Approaches
Scott W. VanderStoep, Deidre D. Johnson, ISBN: 9780470343531, Paperback, 352 pages, 2009. $75.00.

Methods in Educational Research: From Theory to Practice
Marguerite G. Lodico, Dean T. Spaulding, Katherine H. Voegtle, ISBN: 9780787979621, Hardcover, 440 pages, April 2006, $75.00.

SPSS Essentials: Managing and Analyzing Social Sciences Data
John T. Kulas, ISBN: 9780470226179, Paperback, 272 pages, 2008, $45.00.

Quantitative Data Analysis: Doing Social Research to Test Ideas
Donald J. Treiman, ISBN: 9780470380031, Paperback, 480 pages, 2009. $75.00

Mixed Methods in Social Inquiry
Jennifer C. Greene, ISBN: 9780787983826, Paperback, 232 pages, 2007, $45.00.

Action Research Essentials
Dorothy Valcarel Craig, ISBN: 9780470189290, Paperback, 272 pages, 2009. $45.00.

Designing and Constructing Instruments for Social Research and Evaluation
David Colton, Robert W. Covert, ISBN: 9780787987848, Paperback, 412 pages, 2007, $55.00.

AEA members: Take advantage of your 20 percent discount on these titles by ordering at **(877) 762-2974** or **www.josseybass.com** or and entering code **AEAF9.**

JB JOSSEY-BASS™

▸ New and Noteworthy Titles in **Evaluation**

Program Evaluation in Practice: Core Concepts and Examples for Discussion and Analysis
Dean T. Spaulding, ISBN: 9780787986858, Paperback, 176 pages, 2008, $40.00

Evaluation Essentials: Methods For Conducting Sound Research
Beth Osborne Daponte, ISBN: 9780787984397, Paperback, 192 pages, 2008, $60.00.

Evaluation Theory, Models, and Applications
Daniel L. Stufflebeam, Anthony J. Shinkfield, ISBN: 9780787977658, Hardcover, 768 pages, 2007, $70.00.

Logic Modeling Methods in Program Evaluation
Joy A. Frechtling, ISBN: 9780787981969, Paperback, 160 pages, 2007, $48.00.

Evaluator Competencies: Standards for the Practice of Evaluation in Organizations
Darlene F. Russ-Eft, Marcie J. Bober, Ileana de la Teja, Marguerite Foxon, Tiffany A. Koszalka, ISBN: 9780787995997, Hardcover, 240 pages, 2008, $50.00

Youth Participatory Evaluation: Strategies for Engaging Young People
Kim Sabo Flores, ISBN: 9780787983925, Paperback, 208 pages, 2007, $45.00

Performance Evaluation: Proven Approaches for Improving Program and Organizational Performance
Ingrid J. Guerra-López, ISBN: 9780787988838, Paperback, 320 pages, 2008, $45.00

AEA members: Take advantage of your 20 percent discount on these titles by ordering at **(877) 762-2974** or **www.josseybass.com** or and entering code **AEAF9.**